THE
ELEPHANT
IN THE
ROOM

A 22-Day Guide
on How to
Start & Grow
a Super
Successful
Business.

HOW DOES ONE
BECOME SUCCESSFUL?

THIS BOOK
IS 100%
ORGANIC

CLAY CLARK

U.S. SBA Young Entrepreneur of the Year

"MY NAME IS CLAY CLARK AND I WROTE THIS BOOK."

2024

ISBN - 979-8-9899482-6-0

The Elephant in the Room -
How Does One Become Successful?

Published by Clay Clark Publishing

3920 West 91st Street Tulsa South Tulsa, OK 74132

Clay Clark books may be purchased for educational, business or sales promotional use. For more information, please email Clay Clark and his team today at info@thrivetimeshow.com.

CONTENTS

· · · · · · · · · ·

"Clay, you've become an influencer. More than anything else, you have evolved into an influencer where your word has more and more power. As you know, there is a lot of fake influencers out there. I'm glad that you and I agree so much. You are on it, man! Everybody listen to this guy. He knows what he's talking about."

» **ROBERT KIYOSAKI**

(The best-selling author of *The Rich Dad Poor Dad* book series and a man who has sold over 40 million copies of his entrepreneur books.)

"Clay Clark is an entrepreneur extraordinaire."

» **DAVID ROBINSON**

(NBA Hall of Basketball Player, former NBA MVP, NBA Championship Winner, and Investor.)

"[Clay Clark] is like Steve Martin meets Steve Forbes."

» **JIM STOVALL**

(*New York Times* best-selling self-help writer best known for his bestselling novel *The Ultimate Gift*. The book was made into the movie *The Ultimate Gift*, distributed by 20th Century Fox. *The Ultimate Gift* has a prequel called *The Ultimate Life* and a sequel called *The Ultimate Legacy*.)

"I have come to Clay Clark's Thrivetime Show conference/ seminar, and I must say, I didn't know what to expect at first, but it's EXCEPTIONAL. If you are serious, and I mean really serious, about your career, your entrepreneurship, and your wealth creation ability, I strongly, strongly implore you to come to Tulsa, and invest the two days. It will change your life. It's quite extraordinary, and I'm a tough grader."

» **MICHAEL LEVINE**

(The publicist and public relations expert of choice for 58 Academy Award winners, 34 Grammy Award winners, and 43 *New York Times* best-sellers including Michael Jackson, Barbra Streisand, Prince, Nike, and others.)

 FUN FACT: CLAY CLARK'S THRIVETIMESHOW PODCAST HAS HIT #1 ON THE ITUNES PODCAST CHART SIX TIMES

"We've met some of the biggest CEOs in the world, guys that run the biggest Fortune 500 companies, and Clay Clark has 100 times the backbone of the toughest person that you will see."

» **ERIC TRUMP**

(The Executive Vice President of The Trump Organization who is responsible for managing the $8 billion business, thousands of employees, the Trump Organization's real estate, and the Trump brands.)

"IN A CROWDED MARKETPLACE, FITTING IN IS FAILING. IN A BUSY MARKETPLACE, NOT STANDING OUT IS THE SAME AS BEING INVISIBLE."
– SETH GODIN

(Seth Godin is an iconic entrepreneur, best-selling author of 18 books including Purple Cow, and the man who in 1998 sold his company Yoyodyne to Yahoo! for $30 million dollars.)

"IF I HAVE SEEN FARTHER, IT IS BECAUSE I HAVE BEEN ABLE TO STAND ON THE SHOULDERS OF GIANTS."
– SIR ISAAC NEWTON

(Sir Isaac Newton was an English polymath active as a mathematician, physicist, astronomer, alchemist, theologian, and author who was described in his time as a natural philosopher.)

INTRODUCTION

. . . .

Your business is only successful if you sell a product or service to your ideal and likely customers in a sustainable and profitable way that creates both time and financial freedom for you as the owner of the business. A business exists to solve problems for your ideal and likely buyers while producing a sustainable profit for you as a business owner. A successful business is able to provide you and your family the time freedom and financial freedom needed to thrive, and to pursue that which you believe God wants you to pursue!!! A successful business is not an unprofitable hobby that sucks up all of your time and all of your money.

NOTABLE QUOTABLE

"Cherish your visions and your dreams as they are the children of your soul, the blueprints of your ultimate achievements."

» **NAPOLEON HILL**

(The man whom I named my son after, and the man who was mentored directly by the steel tycoon Andrew Carnegie, the best-selling self-help author of all time, during his lifetime, the author of *Think & Grow Rich*, *The Law of Success*, *The Master-Key to Riches*, ect...)

Welcome to ***A Millionaire's Guide to Business Startup Success: The Rush to Revenue & the Proven Path to Sustainable Success & The Elephant In The Room Men's Grooming Lounge Success Story!*** I'm writing this book to help you to learn the specific steps that you must take in order to start and launch a successful business. However, before we get into the practical specific steps that you must take in order to start a successful (profitable) business, I want to teach you the mindset that you must embrace in route to building a successful business.

YOU MUST DECIDE THAT YOU ARE GOING TO GO ALL IN FOR THE NEXT 22 DAYS! You must understand if you do things half-ass your whole life will be terrible. You must be obsessively hungry for success or you will lose! To get into the same mindset with you, as I write this book for you I am personally going to take the next 22 days to only eat two meals a day, to only eat meat, and to only drink water or coffee. Why?

Because that is the kind of ALL-IN MENTALITY that is required to achieve success. Embracing the proven CARNIVORE DIET created by Thrivetime Show Conference Speaker and Podcast Guest, Doctor and Orthopedic Surgeon Shawn Baker, MD sounds extreme, yet it is effective!

"EAT THE BIGGEST FROG FIRST"
-BRIAN TRACY
(The legendary best-selling author, sales trainer,
business growth consultant and keynote success speaker.)

FUN FACT: CLAY CLARK'S THRIVETIMESHOW PODCAST
HAS HIT #1 ON THE ITUNES PODCAST CHART SIX TIMES

NOTABLE QUOTABLE

....

"Remember that your dominating thoughts attract, through a definite law of nature, by the shortest and most convenient route, their physical counterpart. Be careful what your thoughts dwell upon."

» NAPOLEON HILL

(A man who was mentored directly by the steel tycoon Andrew Carnegie, the best-selling self-help author of all-time during his lifetime, the author of *Think & Grow Rich, The Law of Success, The Master-Key to Riches,* etc...)

When you tell your friends and family that you are implementing A Millionaire's Guide to Business Startup Success, they will say that you are being EXTREME. When your friends and family tell you that you are being EXTREME, they are correct, because by default nearly everybody on the planet is EXTREMELY POOR AND NOT SUCCESSFUL which is EXTREMELY CONCERNING to me, but not for most people. In fact, in America today according to USDebtClock.org, as of April 28th 2024, the United States has a population of 336,361,276 and just 9,735,959 classify themselves as self-employed. That means in America today, under 3% of the overall United States population is self employed. Think about that. That is an EXTREME concept.

FUN FACT:

....

"96% of Businesses Fail within 10 Years."

https://www.inc.com/bill-carmody/why-96-of-businesses-fail-within-10-years.html

Inc. Magazine reports 96% of businesses will fail within 10 years. This means that only 4% of the less than 3% of the overall population will become successful by default. What is 4% of 3%? Do the math.

To look at it another way:

FACT #1 - 9,735,959 are self-employed in America.

FACT #2 - Under 400,000 people are successful self-employed people in America out of a population of 336,361,276.

FACT #3 - By default and without implementing the proven processes and success strategies I am teaching in this book, you have approximately a 1 out of 999 chance of succeeding in America today.

"Your only limitation is the one which you set up in your own mind."

» **NAPOLEON HILL**

(A man who was mentored directly by the steel tycoon Andrew Carnegie, the best-selling self-help author of all-time during his lifetime, the author of *Think & Grow Rich, The Law of Success, The Master-Key to Riches*, etc...)

Thus, YOU and I MUST COME INTO AGREEMENT that by default, being successful in America is abnormal, and EXTREME.

DEFINITIONS MATTER:

Extreme:

Furthest from the center or a given point; outermost. Reaching a high or the highest degree; very great.

My friend, I am extremely passionate about your success, thus I need you to get extremely passionate about your goals for a moment so you will find the desire that is required to achieve those EXTREME results you have been searching for.

What are your F7 goals? What are the goals you have for your faith, family, finances, fitness, friendship, fun, and focused attention? Take a moment and be EXTREME and actually write your goals down in this book in the space provided below:

What are your faith goals for this year?

_____

_____

_____

What are your family goals for this year?

_____

_____

_____

What are your financial goals for this year?

_____

_____

_____

What are your fitness goals for this year?

_____

_____

_____

What are your friendship goals for this year?

_____

_____

_____

What are your fun goals for this year?

_____

_____

_____

What are your focused attention goals for this year?

_____

_____

_____

FUN FACT: CLAY CLARK'S THRIVETIMESHOW PODCAST
HAS HIT #1 ON THE ITUNES PODCAST CHART SIX TIMES

If you need more time, that is fine. Actually invest the time needed to write out your goals while I sip on some cold-black coffee and ponder the fact that the next 44 meals that I am going to eat are going to consist of steak, cold-black coffee, and water.

STEP 1 -
Only eat meat.

STEP 2 -
Only drink coffee or water.

STEP 3 -
Don't eat anything other than meat.

STEP 4 -
Don't drink anything other than coffee or water.

"CREATE A DEFINITE PLAN FOR CARRYING OUT YOUR DESIRE AND BEGIN AT ONCE, WHETHER YOU READY OR NOT, TO PUT THIS PLAN INTO ACTION."
- NAPOLEON HILL

WHAT SOLUTION WILL YOU PROVIDE THE WORLD IN EXCHANGE FOR THE MONEY YOU SEEK?

1. Invest the time needed to find and solve a problem that consumers have and are willing to pay for.

2. Invest as much time as needed until you find an existing product or service that you could compete within the marketplace in a differentiated way.

What Problems Can You Solve?

_____

_____

_____

_____

_____

_____

With What Product or Service Can You Compete?

_____

_____

_____

_____

_____

_____

FUN FACT: CLAY CLARK'S THRIVETIMESHOW PODCAST HAS HIT #1 ON THE ITUNES PODCAST CHART SIX TIMES

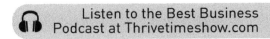

DAY 1

FINDING A PROBLEM TO SOLVE

· · · · · · ·

Thus far today I have eaten steak, cold black coffee, and water and thus far you should be about 10 minutes into this book. It's time for you to take EXTREME ownership for your future success and to 100% mentally commit to knocking out all ,f the action items I will teach you over the next 90 days.

Now it's time for you to establish your revenue goals. The reason a business exists is to create both time and financial freedom for you as the owner of a business in exchange for the problems that you solve for your ideal and likely buyers. What? Let me explain that in a different way. This might sound extreme, but there are essentially just 4 steps to implementing the EXTREME and proven path to successful entrepreneurship:

STEP 1 - Find a problem that real people on the planet earth want to solve.

STEP 2 - Create a solution that real people on the planet are willing to pay to have solved.

STEP 3 - Sell your solution, product or service to your ideal and likely buyers in exchange for a profit.

STEP 4 - Nail it and scale it. And do this over and over until YOU have earned copious amounts of profit.

YOUR BUSINESS EXISTS TO SOLVE PROBLEMS FOR YOU AND YOUR CUSTOMERS.
- CLAY CLARK
(Founder of ThriveTimeShow.com, former U.S. SBA Entrepreneur of the Year, host of the ThriveTime Show, and America's #1 Business Coach.)

When I started the Elephant In the Room Men's Grooming Lounge 13 years ago I pondered the following things:

STEP 1 - What is the problem we are solving? Men in Tulsa, Oklahoma do not have a service provider available that provides a quality haircut while offering a man-focused high-end country club style atmosphere.

STEP 2 - What is the solution we are offering? I started Elephant In the Room Men's Grooming lounge to offer men of Tulsa a quality haircut in a high-end country club style atmosphere.

LEARN HOW TO START AND GROW A BUSINESS BY LISTENING TO THE THRIVETIMESHOW.COM PODCAST TODAY!

STEP 3 - How much will we charge for the solution, services, and products we are going to offer? I sat down with myself and did the math. I determined that if we could make a profit of approximately 20% per haircut then we could have a viable business.

STEP 4 - How can we nail it and scale it? In order to start Elephant In the Room I developed the following aspects of the business listed below. In order for YOU to become a successful entrepreneur you must learn how to master the following business development areas and more:

1. How to name the business.

2. How to create the logo.

3. How to develop the branding.

4. How to develop the business cards.

5. How to develop the marketing print pieces.

6. How to develop a website that wows.

7. How to optimize the website to dominate the search engine results.

8. How to create social media advertisements that generate leads.

9. How to create online retargeting advertisements that follow your website visitors around the internet.

10. How to develop social proof via real client testimonials.

11. How to develop social proof via public relations and media appearances.

12. How to develop social proof through celebrity endorsements.

13. How to develop in-bound calls scripts.

14. How to develop out-bound sales scripts.

15. How to develop the linear workflow for the actual men's grooming services that we provide.

16. How to create an atmosphere with the right overall image and ambiance that our ideal and likely buyers would appreciate.

17. How to generate leads (first time customers who will try out Elephant In The Room Men's Grooming Lounge Experience).

18. How to convert leads into paying customers.

19. How to hire new employees.

20. How to inspire new employees.

21. How to train employees.

22. How to retain employees.

23. How to price the products we offer.

24. How to price the services that we offer.

25. How to create packaging for our customers that purchase products.

26. How to develop the music playlist and overall musical ambiance to create an upbeat men's grooming lounge experience.

27. How to develop a proforma (a projection of future financial performance based upon known variables).

28. How to develop a linear documented workflow that is scalable.

29. How to find a physical location for the high-end men's grooming lounge.

30. How to build out a location.

31. How to manage the contractors that are building out the location.

32. How to fund the creation of the store (I paid cash).

33. How to lead a team.

34. How to lead weekly meetings.

35. How to manage a staff of employees and how to hold employees accountable.

36. How to deal with people within the company who chose to cheat on their spouse.

37. How to deal with people within the company who chose to use the company credit card for personal expenses.

38. How to deal with people within the company who chose to date employees while managing them.

39. How to deal with people within the company who chose to buy a company vehicle without approval.

40. How to deal with people within the company who chose to attempt to promote their mistress into a management position.

41. How to manage people that choose to be chronically late.

42. How to manage people that refuse to use a to-do list.

43. How to manage people that refuse to use a calendar and the concept of time blocking.

44. How to build a checklist for everything.

NOTABLE QUOTABLE

"Every time I read a management or self-help book, I find myself saying, "That's fine, but that wasn't really the hard thing about the situation." The hard thing isn't setting a big, hairy, audacious goal. The hard thing is laying people off when you miss the big goal. The hard thing isn't hiring great people. The hard thing is when those "great people" develop a sense of entitlement and start demanding unreasonable things. The hard thing isn't setting up an organizational chart. The hard thing is getting people to communicate within the organization that you just designed. The hard thing isn't dreaming big. The hard thing is waking up in the middle of the night in a cold sweat when the dream turns into a nightmare."

» BEN HOROWITZ

(The founder of OpsWare which he sold to Hewlett Packard $1.2 and the best-selling author of *The Hard Thing About Hard Things: Building a Business When There Are No Easy Answers* who has now become a well-known venture capitalist.)

 FUN FACT: CLAY CLARK'S THRIVETIMESHOW PODCAST HAS HIT #1 ON THE ITUNES PODCAST CHART SIX TIMES

This might sound extreme, but there are essentially just 4 steps to successfully implementing the EXTREME and proven path to successful weight loss on the **Carnivore Diet**:

STEP 1 -
Only eat meat..

STEP 2 -
Only drink coffee or water..

STEP 3 -
Don't eat anything other than meat..

STEP 4 -
Don't drink anything other than coffee or water..

Remember, in business and in life, simplicity scales and complexity fails.

As an entrepreneur you must master the rhythm of entrepreneurship. This is a rhythm most people will never understand. It goes like this.

STEP 1 - Define what you think is going to work.

STEP 2 - Act after you have gathered the facts and calculated the risks.

STEP 3 - Measure the results.

STEP 4 - Refine and improve until your business is sustainably profitable.

Most people spend their whole lives trying never to make a mistake because it may make them look bad. Most people will never start a business because they have a fear of failing. Most people are simply so consumed with wondering what others will think that they simply do not have the ability to take action. I would argue most people spend their lives trying to buy things they cannot afford to impress people they do not know.

NOTABLE QUOTABLE

"The capacity to surmount failure without being discouraged is the chief asset of every person who attains outstanding success in any calling."

» **NAPOLEON HILL**

(A man who was mentored directly by the steel tycoon Andrew Carnegie, the best-selling self-help author of all-time during his lifetime, the author of *Think & Grow Rich, The Law of Success, The Master-Key to Riches*, etc...)

My friend, you must master this basic mindset and set of principles while reminding yourself, most people are wrong most of the time about most things related to entrepreneurship because most people in America are not successful.

"75% of employees steal from the workplace."

» **U.S. CHAMBER**

"85% of employees lie on resumes."

» **INC. MAGAZINE**

LEARN HOW TO START AND GROW A BUSINESS BY LISTENING TO THE THRIVETIMESHOW.COM PODCAST TODAY!

Again, it's worth repeating here. *Inc. Magazine* reports 96% of businesses will fail within 10 years. This means that only 4% of the less than 3% of the overall population will become successful by default.

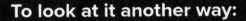

To look at it another way:

FACT #1 - 9,735,959 people are self-employed in America.

FACT #2 - Under 400,000 people are successful self-employed people in America out of a population of 336,361,276.

FACT #3 - By default and without implementing the proven processes and success strategies I am teaching in this book, you have approximately a 1 out of 999 chance of succeeding in America today.

You will be successful, but you must master the basics of entrepreneurship. Now, if you will excuse me, I'm going to contemplate eating meat and drinking coffee. Remember, simplicity scales, and complexity fails.

NOTABLE QUOTABLE

"Don't allow yourself to concede to eating food full of cheap grain, sugar, and highly processed oils. Take charge of your health and give your body what it needs: meat!"

» **DOCTOR SHAWN BAKER**
(Best-selling author of *The Carnivore Diet* and legendary Joe Rogan Podcast guest.)

Quick Note:

Always keep in mind that soon and very soon you are going to have to sell a solution to your ideal and likely buyers in exchange for a profit because unless you can sell, your business will go to hell.

Time freedom and financial freedom will only be created once you master the art of scalably selling solutions, products, and services to your ideal and likely buyers in exchange for a profit.

LEARN HOW TO START AND GROW A BUSINESS BY LISTENING
TO THE THRIVETIMESHOW.COM PODCAST TODAY!

19

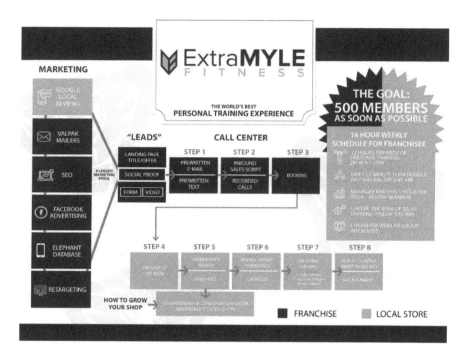

FUN FACT: CLAY CLARK'S THRIVETIMESHOW PODCAST
HAS HIT #1 ON THE ITUNES PODCAST CHART SIX TIMES

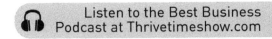
DAY 2

MASTERING THE RHYTHM OF ENTREPRENEURSHIP

. . . .

In order to succeed as an entrepreneur you must develop the habit of over-delivering and exceeding the expectations of each and every customer that you have the opportunity to deliver a product or service to. This must become your normal. You must learn to 'wow' your customers.

1. You must aim to show up early for every meeting and to over-deliver the level of quality you deliver to each and every customer you provide services and products to!

2. You must deliver the products and services to your customers faster than you promised.

3. You must deliver the products and services to your customers in a way that exceeds their expectations.

4. You must dress the way you want to be addressed.

5. You must create a decor in your office that makes your customers want to hang around for more.

6. You must be intentional about the smells in your office and the smells your

21

customers experience when they do business with you.

7. You must be intentional about the music you play in your office and that music must create an atmosphere that wows your customers.

8. You must aim to WOW each and every customer NOW.

9. Your packaging must blow the minds of your customers.

10. The food you serve must be first-class.

11. Your business cards must be first class or nothing.

12. Every aspect of your business must be the best or nothing.

13. Your website must wow!

14. The "About Us" video on your website must wow.

15. Remember, if you are half-ass your whole life will be terrible.

16. You must install mystery shoppers within your business that will objectively and honestly let you know how you stack up versus the competition.

NOTABLE QUOTABLE

"You can start right where you stand and apply the habit of going the extra mile by rendering more service and better service than you are now being paid for."

» **NAPOLEON HILL**

(A man who was mentored directly by the steel tycoon Andrew Carnegie, the best-selling self-help author of all-time during his lifetime, the author of *Think & Grow Rich, The Law of Success, The Master-Key to Riches*, etc...)

NOTABLE QUOTABLE

"If you give someone a present, and you give it to them in a Tiffany box, it's likely that they'll believe the gift has higher perceived value than if you gave it to them in no box or a box of less prestige. That's not because the receiver of the gift is a fool. But instead, because we live in a culture in which we gift wrap everything — our politicians, our corporate heads, our movie and TV stars, and even our toilet paper. Public Relations is like gift wrapping."

» **MICHAEL LEVINE**

(Michael Levine is the publicist and public relations expert of choice for 58 Academy Award winners, 34 Grammy Award winners, and 43 *New York Times* best-sellers including Michael Jackson, Barbra Streisand, Prince, Nike, and others.)

Quick Reminder: If you want to stand out in the cluttered world of commerce, you must learn to over-deliver. You must embrace the belief that if you are half-ass your whole life will be terrible. You must aim to wow or nothing. In the upcoming chapters I am going to teach you the specific strategies and super moves you can use to start and grow a successful company, but nothing will work unless you do. You must WOW your customers NOW! If you don't have any customers yet, start by wowing your boss. Show up to work early. Dress to impress. Exceed the expectations your boss has for you. Beat your deadlines and find a way to knock out your projects under budget! When you WOW, you will stand out NOW in a world where mediocrity is the norm.

And yes, this mindset of over-delivering might sound EXTREME, but YOU must remember that most Americans are EXTREMELY POOR by default, and I find this to be EXTREMELY CONCERNING.

Back to the Carnivore Diet. The challenging thing about being on the Carnivore Diet for the past 24 hours is to remember I am on the Carnivore Diet: no sweeteners, no fruit, just meat.

This might sound extreme, but there are essentially just 4 steps to successfully implementing the EXTREME and proven path to successful weight loss on the Carnivore Diet:

STEP 1 -
Only eat meat..

STEP 2 -
Only drink coffee or water..

STEP 3 -
Don't eat anything other than meat..

STEP 4 -
Don't drink anything other than coffee or water..

"ALL THE SMILES IN THE WORLD AREN'T GOING TO HELP YOU IF YOUR PRODUCT OR SERVICE IS NOT WHAT THE CUSTOMER WANTS."
-THE SERVICE PROFIT CHAIN

NOTABLE QUOTABLE

"Mastery is not about being special or more gifted than anyone else. Mastery is a direct result of pigheaded discipline and determination."

» CHET HOLMES

(The legendary business consultant, business growth coach and the best-selling author of *The Ultimate Sales Machine*.)

Quick Note:

Soon and very soon you are going to have to sell a solution to your ideal and likely buyers in exchange for a profit because unless you can sell, your business will go to hell.

"ONLY WORK VIA APPOINTMENT."
– CLAY CLARK

(Founder of ThriveTimeShow.com, former U.S. SBA
Entrepreneur of the Year, host of the ThriveTime Show,
and America's #1 Business Coach.)

FUN FACT: CLAY CLARK'S THRIVETIMESHOW PODCAST
HAS HIT #1 ON THE ITUNES PODCAST CHART SIX TIMES

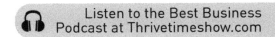

Listen to the Best Business
Podcast at Thrivetimeshow.com

DAY 3

USE A CALENDAR & TO-DO LIST AT ALL TIMES

Successful people know where they are going, when they are going, and they know what needs to be done. However, most people don't know where they are going, when they are going and what needs to be done.

NOTABLE QUOTABLE

"Begin with the end in mind."

» **STEPHEN COVEY**

(The best-selling author of *The 7 Habits of Highly Effective People, First Things First, The 8th Habit,* and many other top success books, etc. He was a professor at the Jon M. Huntsman School of Business at Utah State University (USU) at the time of his death.)

Starting TODAY, you must use a to-do list and a calendar at all times. If you think of a "BIG IDEA" write it down. If you have a "BIG IDEA" that pops into your head, write it down. It is absolutely important you develop the habit of carrying a to-do list and a calendar at all times because everything impacts everything.

Having coached thousands of business owners to success, I have noticed a massive GAP in the productivity of the clients that have a to-do list and a calendar and those who do not. Stop double-booking yourself, forgetting to do something or trying to remember that "BIG IDEA" you had yesterday. Get a to-do list and a calendar today. Every single day to date, I start my day two hours before I interact with my employees and clients by organizing my to-do list and calendar.

NOTABLE QUOTABLE

"The world has the habit of making room for the man whose words and actions show that he knows where he is going."

» **NAPOLEON HILL**

(The best-selling self-help author of his time and the man who wrote the legendary self-help classic, *Think & Grow Rich*. I named by son after Napoleon Hill because Napoleon Hill's writings changed my life.)

To demonstrate the importance of maintaining an updated to-do list and calendar I am going to insert today's calendar into this book below. It would be absolutely impossible for me to remember what I am supposed to do today even if I tried. That is why I use a calendar. The pen is for remembering and the mind is for thinking. Stop wasting your mental capacity on trying to remember what you are supposed to be doing today.

"ALL THE SMILES IN THE WORLD AREN'T GOING
TO HELP YOU IF YOUR PRODUCT OR SERVICE IS
NOT WHAT THE CUSTOMER WANTS."
–THE SERVICE PROFIT CHAIN

This is an actual look at my calendar.

6:00 - Nathan - Complete Carpet -
6 – 7am

Clay meets with the coaches
7 – 8am

Elephant in the Room Management
8 – 9am

Clay meets with | Paul Sullins sits
9 – 10am | 9 – 10am

Clay meets with Kenny & Highway
10 – 11am

Clay Calls Papagallos - 321-4
11am – 12pm
11:15 AM - Clay

13 Point Assessment / Wes | ALFA

13 Point Assessment / Interview -

Doctor Shawn Ba | Clay meets with
1 – 2pm
Clay meets with

Clay interviews Peter Taunton - CC

Interview Availability - CC, 2:30pm

3:00 PM - Clay interviews Dr. Mark

Clay is interviewed on Laura Lynn L

Clay interviews Matt Kline - CC, 4p

Clay is interviewed on Blessed to T

Clay works On Big Project - CC
5 – 6pm

As an entrepreneur, you must do things differently from most people and you must become a productive, organized, and self-disciplined person.

Statistically speaking, by default success is not likely to be achieved on the planet earth. Remember in America today, we have a population of 336,118,791 people and just 9,049,862 are self-employed.

Remember, *Inc. Magazine* reports 96% of businesses will fail within 10 years, which means only 4% of 2.69% of the overall population will become successful by default.

To look at it another way:

FACT #1 - 9,735,959 are self-employed in America.

FACT #2 - Under 400,000 people are successful self-employed people in America out of a population of 336,361,276.

FACT #3 - By default and without implementing the proven processes and success strategies I am teaching in this book, you have approximately a 1 out of 999 chance of succeeding in America today.

You must choose to live abnormally if you want to experience abnormal results. Mediocre minds are always saying self-defeating statements such as:

1. You don't need to work so hard.

2. If it is meant to be it will happen.

3. Don't force it.

4. You only live once, don't work so hard.

5. You are Type-A, calm down and stop carrying that to-do list everywhere.

6. What is your problem, why does everything need to be so organized?

7. You are so uptight, you don't have to organize everything in your office.

"EXPECT MORE THAN OTHERS THINK POSSIBLE."
- HOWARD SCHULTZ (FOUNDER OF STARBUCKS)

My friend, as you begin to master these FOUNDATIONAL SUPER MOVES, SUCCESS STRATEGIES, and PROVEN PROCESSES you will be prepared to achieve massive success. However, if you don't master these FOUNDATIONAL PRINCIPLES, the business you are building will collapse as you attempt to build a BIG ORGANIZATION on top of a foundation of perpetual DISORGANIZATION.

NOTABLE QUOTABLE

"We must all suffer from one of two pains: the pain of discipline or the pain of regret. The difference is discipline weighs ounces while regret weighs tons."

» **JIM ROHN**

(The legendary entrepreneur, best-selling author, speaker, trainer and business growth coach.)

Now, back to the Carnivore Diet. Thus far, I'm down 4 pounds in days and all I am eating is meat. Is it fun eating only meat? No. Is it exciting eating only meat? No. Is there endless variety in only eating meat? No. The challenging thing about being on the Carnivore Diet for the past 48 hours is to remember to only eat meat. No sweeteners, no fruit, just meat.

This might sound extreme, but there are essentially just 4 steps to successfully implementing the EXTREME and proven path

STEP 1 -
Only eat meat..

STEP 2 -
Only drink coffee or water..

STEP 3 -
Don't eat anything other than meat..

STEP 4 -
Don't drink anything other than coffee or water..

to successful weight loss on the Carnivore Diet:

NOTABLE QUOTABLE

"The difference between a fixed mindset and a growth mindset is the difference between being stuck in place and moving forward towards your goals."

» **DOCTOR SHAWN BAKER**

(Best-selling author of *The Carnivore Diet* and legendary Joe Rogan Podcast guest.)

"Discipline is the bridge between goals and accomplishment."

» **JIM ROHN**

(The legendary entrepreneur, best-selling author, speaker, trainer and business growth coach.)

EXAMPLE TO-DO LIST

- Call Jonathan - Revolution - Pause his Indeed Advertisements
- Call Jonathan - Thrivetime Show Testimonials - Add this video https://www.youtube.com/watch?v=brRXjUTp15Q&t=1s to this page https://www.thrivetimeshow.com/testimonials/ (replace their previous testimonial)
- Call Will - 24/7 Disaster - About adding 100 articles per month - would like to see disasterherotulsa.com on the keywords list for companies also. Thanks.
- Call the Roads Church - I still have a question about Relentless. although the Relentless page doesn't show up, it still shows under the list of ministries. How do I make it disappear from that list? (I have attached a screenshot of what I am talking about.
- DEEP DIVE - Write questions for Dan Schawbel - Interviewing 12/10
- DEEP DIVE - Write questions for Nick Symmonds - Interviewing 12/12
- DEEP DIVE - Write questions for Brad Lomenick - Interviewing on 12/19
- DEEP DIVE - Write questions for Pastor Larry Osborne - Interviewing on 1/9
- DEEP DIVE - Write questions for Kevin Kelly - Interviewing on 12/18
- DEEP DIVE - Call Wendy - https://docs.google.com/document/d/1savibPtgfhkFDrpsFROe91zPDxx8Zse3Eis1sSVW4iM/edit?usp=sharing
- Call Vanessa - Charge Tim Redmond for PettisBuilders.com and add to client roster
- Call Vanessa - Verify we are charging Tim Redmond for Electric Techs
- Deep Dive - Thrivetime Show - Write questions for Pastor Randy Frazee
- DEEP DIVE - Thrivetime Show - Write questions for Jon Gordon - https://docs.google.com/document/d/1uvGi7OAwPrP1J6oQJlKZuhYocXFrGLjgoSaCZOibG6Y/edit?usp=sharing - Interviewing 12/18/18
- DEEP DIVE - Thrivetime Show - Write the questions for Andy Bernstein - https://docs.google.com/document/d/151Uo3d3ldxp_gC3SpMDB2XdIlmrWT6A_LeX1frEetok/edit?usp=sharing - Interviewing 12/17
- DEEP DIVE - Thrivetime Show - Write the questions for Jeff Bethke - if we can talk about our family teams venture (parenting and family resources) that'd be great - Interviewing 12/13
- DEEP DIVE - Thrivetimeshow - Write questions for Dan Millman (See Brady Boyd questions) - https://docs.google.com/document/d/1BFCa_HtPxPqyx5tn9lRapYBy8qhEs5OBdKcJ_wzoiO0/edit?usp=sharing - Interviewing 12/11
- Call Sidney - Confirm Christmas Party details with Sydney 2. Call Marshall to confirm the details for Christmas Party
- Call Vanessa Provide the following documents for One Fire Meeting - https://docs.google.com/document/d/1d-Ng3KUNPpQDJC1R2waJIXAU4aMSG38rcPUGViaSs2E/edit?usp=sharing
- DEEP DIVE - Edit Score Bball Book - https://docs.google.com/document/d/1PyKf5IbBy2DQz_xkASOILI132Ks9Mirl2GzfQMzUYc/edit?usp=sharing
- Record - Intro Rap Songs (Send over to Jonathan)
- Write Noah letter of recommendation - https://docs.google.com/document/d/1LcKny0eVTUfrNUigyu50K0GYMoxvgP9JG4De9lFmOro/edit?usp=sharing
- Call Syndication Services
- DEEP DIVE - Add to Dream 100 1. Relevant Cultural Product People 2. Add Radio Station Syndication Services
- Call Mac - Oklahoma City - Radio Show
- Home - Add songs to office playlist
- Call Wes - Tip Top K9 - Wes - Begin FDD Process 1. Costs? 2. Timeline
- Call Jonathan - Connect with Vanessa about buying a flip house
- Call Jonathan - Books in the Elephant In The Room Stores (1. Signs for Store 2. Books to Stock 3. Initial Order Amount
- DEEP DIVE - Prune the FDD - https://docs.google.com/document/d/1UD_KIXqKpeuMB9Aut76iH9ivEt1ZRYAkctz3eBQFeEs/edit?usp=sharing
- Clay - Sam Adams - Get Aaron to have Glenn sign the "Request for Issuance of an Active Provisional Sales Associate"
- Record - Kvell - Edit the audio into commercial - Looking forward to hearing your feedback. https://drive.google.com/drive/folders/17mDxqQfoKiJzjPjK3y4RM9_QsG1QobYH?usp=sharing"
- Call Vanessa - Look into buying an ASCAP license
- DEEP DIVE - Create Elephant In The Room - Shadow Itinerary (Plan for every visit) 2. Screens, etc.
- DEEP DIVE - Thom Clark Stories - https://docs.google.com/document/d/1ziYSHWAqxWS9RA8LDHFEqzOAAVRWvA_Fz6juH_Fl9o/edit?usp=sharing
- DEEP DIVE - Yelp Breakdown - https://docs.google.com/document/d/1pwFWEPjV8Api2lakSGjTmE1uy2B_Qdx-rxmTWecoQ-A/edit?usp=sharing
- DEEP DIVE - Elephant In The Room - Create On-Boarding Checklists 2. Discovery Days
- "Record - Kvell - Edit the audio into commercial - Looking forward to hearing your feedback. https://drive.google.com/drive/folders/17mDxqQfoKiJzjPjK3y4RM9_QsG1QobYH?usp=sharing""
- Record - Edit Morgan Freeman Voice over - https://www.dropbox.com/sh/yir9h5iif0g7n2h/AADiMhyY3sbQcwNg0HQgPSBMa?dl=0
- Record - Morgan Freeman Voice over (edited) https://www.dropbox.com/s/sjxlu4dgnpu9zku/Dr.%20Zoeltner%20Named%20Said%20Correctly%20-%20Morgan%20Freeman.mp3?dl=0
- Record - Edit Samuel L Jackson Reads - https://www.dropbox.com/s/oxssuqs0b3u36f/092418ThrivetimeSchool_SamJackson.wav?dl=0
- Call Jonathan - Answering a Thriver question
- Call Jonathan - Review Rashad Jennings questions - https://docs.google.com/document/d/1TcUFue76YXar8mrqBEWN0FyLyxWTdNVis1tidWgaKOvc/edit?usp=sharing
- Call Jonathan - Ordering TLC business cards
- Call Steve - Move Wednesdays from 11 AM to 3 PM for Sam Adams Realty
- Call Kendal with Clay Staires - Recommendation
- Call Joel Wiland - Interview for podcast - Blaine Bartel
- Call Vanessa - Bathroom Fixes - https://docs.google.com/document/d/1vjjl-oihpwB2QXkPyXAEh19zKo-qbhpuHIN8r7uBOKM/edit?usp=sharing
- Call Debbie - Thrive quarterly review - June 1st at 8am
- Call Vanessa - OneFire - Prepare for meeting - https://docs.google.com/spreadsheets/d/1STSFRIxxQ6tStXTNiFiPYYsQVTtalbVJdAPrHGsLgebY/edit?usp=sharing
- Call Tim w FC - https://docs.google.com/spreadsheets/d/1STSFRIxxQ6tStXTNiFiPYYsQVTtalbVJdAPrHGsLgebY/edit?usp=sharing
- DEEP DIVE - The Roads - Audit Praise and Worship Service (Bethel) - 1. https://www.youtube.com/watch?v=xCjH8tL87Os&list=PLNpqb6N1H8V2ZNrt7CjaMgH8Bersc-RAx 2. https://www.youtube.com/watch?v=ZTrBnnSbsfk
- Call Jonathan Barnett - Jack Huffman email
- Call Jonathan Barnett - Download - https://www.dropbox.com/sh/78nahnm0fcar0zh/AAAIllRR3NJszQeCYNgjYJQ-Na?dl=0
- DEEP DIVE - Updated Dream 100 Podcasts - https://docs.google.com/spreadsheets/d/1n-t_GsefPkTnrP-1-6EaVCb0Vjc72i656i-3nfpcfZw/edit?usp=sharing
- Fix Aubrey's laptop
- Call Eric Chupp - Top 5 podcasts on iTunes - https://docs.google.com/document/d/1mJOeQtp8GLf-0UwLpuYTxhKPRKCtxFZGZ_bFDam918/edit?usp=sharing
- Call Jonathan - Create OxiFresh Landing Page on ThrivetimeShow (today, much easier - grab images from new.oxifresh.com
- DEEP DIVE - Elephant - Create Discovery Day Path (see Oxi Fresh Itinerary)
- Call Brian Gibson - Hammer of Deal - 80/10/10 - New LLC
- Call Brian Chalkin - Book a time to meet
- Call KPAM - Chris Kelly - Get into other markets (now we are in Itunes Top 10)
- Call Wes Carter - Order trademark for Sam Adams Realty
- DEEP DIVE - Podcast Book Landing Page Creation
- Call Wes - Do Your Job - Action Steps

Quick Note:

Always keep in mind that soon and very soon you are going to have to sell a solution to your ideal and likely buyers in exchange for a profit because unless you can sell, your business will go to hell.

FUN FACT: CLAY CLARK'S THRIVETIMESHOW PODCAST HAS HIT #1 ON THE ITUNES PODCAST CHART SIX TIMES

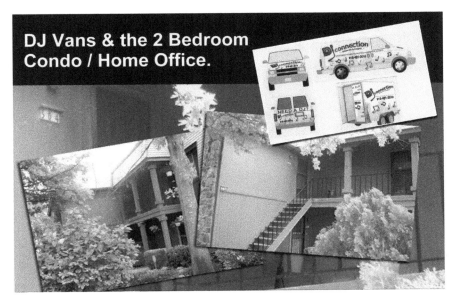

DJ Vans & the 2 Bedroom
Condo / Home Office.

As I was building and scaling my first business
DJconnection.com, I too had to learn how to stay
organized as a result of successfully implementing
calendars and to-do list mastery.

NOTABLE QUOTABLE

"A goal is a dream with a deadline."

> » **NAPOLEON HILL**

(The best-selling self-help author of his time and the
man who wrote the legendary self-help classic, *Think
& Grow Rich*. I named by son after Napoleon Hill
because Napoleon Hill's writings changed my life.)

IT'S NOT ABOUT HOW MUCH YOU MAKE,
ITS ABOUT HOW MUCH YOU KEEP.
-CLAY CLARK

(Founder of ThriveTimeShow.com, former U.S. SBA
Entrepreneur of the Year, host of the ThriveTime Show,
and America's #1 Business Coach.)

FUN FACT: CLAY CLARK'S THRIVETIMESHOW PODCAST
HAS HIT #1 ON THE ITUNES PODCAST CHART SIX TIMES

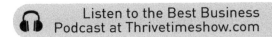

Listen to the Best Business
Podcast at Thrivetimeshow.com

DAY 4

MAKE IT YOUR MISSION TO LIVE BELOW YOUR MEANS

Alright, it's DAY #4 on our journey together as I teach you the proven processes and success strategies you need to learn in order to greatly increase how much you earn! However, you must master this skill and you must master this skill TODAY if you want to achieve massive success. You must develop the habit of saving money and the love for saving money! Most entrepreneurs and business people get very excited when you start talking about their vision, branding, marketing, logos, social media advertising, and wealth. However, very few people get excited about saving money and living below your means!

NOTABLE QUOTABLE

"The difference between great people and everyone else is that great people create their lives actively, while everyone else is created by their lives, passively waiting to see where life takes them next. The difference between the two is living fully and just existing."

» **MICHAEL GERBER**

(Thrivetime Show Podcast guest and the best-selling author of the *E-Myth Revisited.*)

You must get genuinely excited about saving money if you ever wish to achieve MASSIVE financial freedom and success. When I was growing my first business DJConnection.com, I literally tried to live as cheaply as possible. I drove a 1989 hatchback Ford Escort. I ate the 4 for $1 dollar yogurts from Walmart and the Budget Gourmet (a contradiction in terms) Chicken Panini meals found in the frozen food section at Walmart for nearly every meal. My wife and I chose to turn off our air conditioning and our heat in our apartment so we could save money and buy the sound equipment, lighting equipment, and advertising materials we needed to grow DJConnection.com.

NOTABLE QUOTABLE

"Do not save what is left after spending, but spend what is left after saving."

» **WARREN BUFFETT**

(Warren Edward Buffett is an American businessman, investor, and philanthropist who currently serves as the co-founder, chairman, and CEO of Berkshire Hathaway. As a result of his immense investment success, Buffett is one of the best-known investors in the world. As of January 2024, he had a net worth of $122 billion, making him the tenth-richest person in the world.)

I didn't have a rich cousin, a wealthy investor, a bank, a government grant, or some magical financial solution to start and grow DJConnection.com. However, I did choose to live below my means and I chose to not buy things I could not afford to impress people I did not know. Stay focused, keep it simple and choose to live below your means if you want to achieve your dreams.

When starting Elephant In The Room Mens Grooming Lounge, I self-funded the launch of the business and covered the losses as I introduced the Elephant In The Room Lounge to the Tulsa Marketplace.

NOTABLE QUOTABLE

"If you cannot save money, the seeds of greatness are not in you."

» **W. CLEMENT STONE**

(W. Clement Stone was born in Chicago, Illinois, on May 4, 1902. His father died in 1905 leaving his family in debt. In 1908 he hawked newspapers on the South Side of Chicago while his mother worked as a dressmaker. By 1915 he owned his own newsstand. In 1918 he moved to Detroit to sell casualty insurance for his mother. Stone dropped out of high school to sell insurance full-time. He received a diploma from the YMCA Central High School in Chicago. He took courses at *Detroit College of Law* (now, *Michigan State University College of Law*) and *Northwestern University*. Much of what is known about Stone comes from his autobiography *The Success System That Never Fails*.[2] In that book, he tells of his early business life, which started with selling newspapers in restaurants. At the time, this was a novel thing to do, a departure from the typical practice of boys hawking newspapers on street corners.)

In what areas of your life can you dramatically decrease your spending starting now?

Food? _____

Going Out to Eat? _____

Entertainment? _____

Vacations? _____

Your Cable / Internet Bill? _____

Car Payments? _____

Gambling? _____

Drugs? _____

Concerts? _____

Business Lease? _____

Home/Rental Costs? _____

What is an expense that you can reduce starting now so you can afford to save the money needed to achieve success?

_____
_____

I love saving money. As I am writing this now I find myself getting excited about reducing expenses. When I was building Djconnection.com I used to make bets with myself that I could eat every week for only $40.00 total.

NOTABLE QUOTABLE

"A budget is telling your money where to go instead of wondering where it went."

» **DAVE RAMSEY**

(Financial guru, *New York Times* best-selling author and the host of the Dave Ramsey Show.)

To look at it another way:

FACT #1 - 9,735,959 are self-employed in America.

FACT #2 - Under 400,000 people are successful self-employed people in America out of a population of 336,361,276.

FACT #3 - By default and without implementing the proven processes and success strategies I am teaching in this book, you have approximately a 1 out of 999 chance of succeeding in America today.

I am going to repeat this to you EVERYDAY because it is SUPER IMPORTANT that you know this to be true. SUCCESS IS NOT NORMAL. Remember, Inc. Magazine reports 96% of businesses will fail within 10 years, which means only 4% of 2.69% of the overall population will become successful by default.

Now back to that meat only eating thing, called the Carnivore Diet. Yesterday, I interviewed the inventor of The Carnivore Diet, Doctor Shawn Baker and I am now more convinced than ever that I am going to only eat meat for these next 30 days. Thus far, I'm down 4.5 pounds in 4 days and all I am eating is meat. Moderation causes mediocrity and not going all-in creates a whole life of half-assness in business and in every other area of life. The most challenging thing about being on the Carnivore Diet for the past 72 hours is to continue to remember, no sweeteners, no fruit, just meat.

Much like choosing to live below your means, choosing to only eat meat might not be the most fun thing in the world, but it is effective. Knowing there are simply 4 steps to successfully implementing the EXTREME and proven path to successful weight loss on the Carnivore Diet is both mind-freeing and mind-blowing. I think most of us want success to be more complicated.

NOTABLE QUOTABLE

"If you will live like no one else, later you can live like no one else. Pray like it all depends on God, but work like it all depends on you."

» **DAVE RAMSEY**

(Financial guru, *New York Times* best-selling author and the host of the Dave Ramsey Show.)

FUN FACT: CLAY CLARK'S THRIVETIMESHOW PODCAST HAS HIT #1 ON THE ITUNES PODCAST CHART SIX TIMES

STEP 1 -
Only eat meat..

STEP 2 -
Only drink coffee or water..

STEP 3 -
Don't eat anything other than meat..

STEP 4 -
Don't drink anything other than coffee or water..

Quick Note:

In the not so distant future you are going to have to sell a solution to your ideal and likely buyers in exchange for a profit because unless you can sell, your business will go to hell.

LEARN HOW TO START AND GROW A BUSINESS BY LISTENING TO THE THRIVETIMESHOW.COM PODCAST TODAY!

43

"*TIME IS THE SCARCEST RESOURCE OF THE MANAGER;
IF IT IS NOT MANAGED, NOTHING ELSE CAN BE MANAGED.*"
– PETER F. DRUCKER

(The legendary management consultant educator,
and author, whose writings contributed to the
philosophical and practical foundations of modern
management theory. He was also a leader in the
development of management education, and
invented the concepts known as management by
objectives and self-control and he has been described
as "the founder of modern management".)

  FUN FACT: CLAY CLARK'S THRIVETIMESHOW PODCAST
HAS HIT #1 ON THE ITUNES PODCAST CHART SIX TIMES

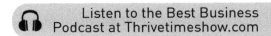
DAY 5

DETERMINE YOUR GOALS, WRITE THEM DOWN & BLOCK OUT TIME TO ACHIEVE THEM

. . . .

Hey, things are looking good. It's day five and if you are reading this, then you are still alive! Now it's time to determine your goals and to block out time to actually achieve them. The entire purpose of creating a business is to create a revenue stream that will create the financial capacity to achieve both the time and financial freedom needed to pursue that which you believe God has called you to do. So if you did have all of the money in the world, what would you ideally spend your day doing? What are your goals for your faith, family, finances, fitness, friendship, and fun?

If you had all of the time in the world, what would you choose to spend your day doing?

Remember, what gets scheduled gets done and what does not get scheduled does not get done. So take out a pen and fill out the following goal and time blocking questionnaire and let's get serious about helping you to turn your dreams into reality starting now.

NOTABLE QUOTABLE

"Nature will not tolerate idleness or vacuums of any sort. All space must be and is filled with something . . . When the individual does not use the brain for the expression of positive, creative thoughts, nature fills the vacuum by forcing the brain to act upon negative thoughts."

» **NAPOLEON HILL**

(A man who was mentored directly by the steel tycoon Andrew Carnegie, the best-selling self-help author of all-time during his lifetime, the author of *Think & Grow Rich, The Law of Success, The Master-Key to Riches*, etc...)

Faith - What are your faith goals and when will you block out time on a weekly recurring basis in your schedule to pursue your faith goals?

_____

_____

Family - What are your family goals and when will you block out time on a weekly recurring basis in your schedule to pursue your family goals?

_____

_____

Finances - What are your financial goals and when will you block out time on a weekly recurring basis in your schedule to pursue your financial goals?

_____

_____

Fitness - What are your fitness goals and when will you block out time on a weekly recurring basis in your schedule to pursue your fitness goals?

_____

_____

Friendship - What are your friendship goals and when will you block out time on a weekly recurring basis in your schedule to pursue your friendship goals?

_____

_____

Fun - What are your faith goals and when will you block out time on a weekly recurring basis in your schedule to pursue your fun goals?

_____

_____

NOTABLE QUOTABLE

"Every adversity brings with it the seed of an equivalent advantage."

» **NAPOLEON HILL**

(A man who was mentored directly by the steel tycoon Andrew Carnegie, the best-selling self-help author of all-time during his lifetime, the author of *Think & Grow Rich, The Law of Success, The Master-Key to Riches*, etc...)

Having worked with thousands of clients to help them turn their goals into reality, I have become a master of time blocking and great observer of the fact that what gets scheduled gets done, and those who actually take the time needed to block out time for the pursuit of the goals they have for their faith, family, finances, fitness, friendship, and fun are the most happy and the most successful. Need a place to start? Want to see an example? Listed below is my schedule for this week.

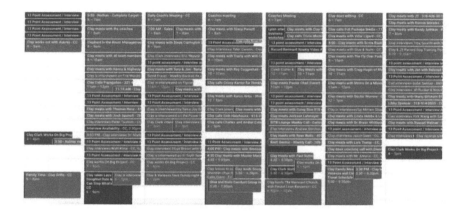

It's OK for you to judge me and my schedule and to say I am not blocking out enough time for what matters most, but it's not OK for you to not judge yourself as well. You need to get serious about TIME BLOCKING and TIME BLOCKING NOW because no one drifts to success. You must make it your top priority to define your goals and block out the time needed for the achievement of your goals. Make sure you are setting goals that motivate you, that fire you up, and that make you want to leap out of bed each morning eager to turn those goals and dreams into reality.

NOTABLE QUOTABLE

"You don't have to be great to start, but you have to start to be great."

» ZIG ZIGLAR

(Hilary Hinton "Zig" Ziglar was an American author, salesman, sales trainer, success coach and motivational speaker.)

Now the trade-off of being a super diligent and high-performing person is that you can no longer be a drifter, you can no longer be a slacker who is aimlessly drifting through life and doing nothing most of the time. So in order to become super successful, you are going to have to stop doing certain activities. Make a list of the activities that you will stop engaging in beginning now in order to create the time needed to achieve massive success.

NOTABLE QUOTABLE

"Mastery is not about being special or more gifted than anyone else. Mastery is a direct result of pigheaded discipline and determination".

» Chet Holmes

(The legendary business consultant, business growth coach, and the best-selling author of *The Ultimate Sales Machine*.)

- ⊘ Stop watching TV.
- ⊘ Stop scrolling through social media.
- ⊘ Stop going out to eat every night.
- ⊘ Stop gossiping with friends at the local coffee shop.
- ⊘ Stop going on endless vacations.
- ⊘ Stop spending time with urgent, emotional, and nefarious people.
- ⊘ Stop focusing on things you can't control.

DESIGN THE LIFE YOU WANT

Today, take out your calendar and write into your schedule the hours that you are willing to work on the various F7 aspects of your life (as an example, I will not work on Sundays, unless it is a super rare occasion).

Write out the boundaries with your time and schedule that you are not willing to cross. As an example, when I first started my businesses, I was willing to work every hour of every day Monday through Sunday. Now, I will not meet people for lunch, attend work related parties, go out to dinner with clients, or ever leave my office during the workday. I turn my phone off every weekend, all weekend and I don't return calls of any kind that relate to work on the weekends.

Create one master calender that includes your work life & personal life...in 1 hour time blocks.

Boundary 1: _____

Boundary 2: _____

Boundary 3: _____

Boundary 4: _____

Boundary 5: _____

We all only have 24 hours per day and if you want to become a business startup success, you must become a master of time blocking. You must learn to say NO if you want to grow. You must learn to say NO to distractions and time-wasting actions if you ever want to gain traction in achieving your goals.

FUN FACT: CLAY CLARK'S THRIVETIMESHOW PODCAST HAS HIT #1 ON THE ITUNES PODCAST CHART SIX TIMES

Now back to becoming the "Carnivore King." Last night I took my kids out for dinner at a local restaurant after we watched our middle daughter compete in cheerleading. When we sat down at Outback the wonderful waitress asked me if I wanted bread and I said "No." You know why? I said "NO" because I have mentally committed myself to only eating meat. Two days ago, as I mentioned, I interviewed the inventor of The Carnivore Diet, Doctor Shawn Baker and I am now more convinced than ever that I am going to only eat meat for these next 30 days!!!! Thus far, I'm down 4.6 pounds in just 4 days and all I am eating is meat. The most difficult thing about this Carnivore Diet is obsessively remembering that I am on the carnivore diet. I must say no. I must mentally prepare myself to say no to even good things so I can say yes to implementing the carnivore diet. No sweeteners, no fruit, just meat.

NOTABLE QUOTABLE

"Drifting, without aim or purpose, is the first cause of failure."

» **NAPOLEON HILL**

(The best-selling author of *Think & Grow Rich* and a man considered to be the best-selling self-help author in the history of self-help books.)

Much like choosing to live below your means, choosing to eat only meat might not be the most fun thing in the world, but it is effective. Knowing there are simply 4 steps to successfully implementing the EXTREME and proven path to successful loss on the Carnivore Diet is mind-freeing and terrifying because once you know exactly what to do, you no longer have the excuse of "I didn't know."

STEP 1 -

Only eat meat..

STEP 2 -

Only drink coffee or water..

STEP 3 -

Don't eat anything other
than meat..

STEP 4 -

Don't drink anything other
than coffee or water..

Quick Note:

*Always keep in mind that soon and very soon
you are going to have to sell a solution to your
ideal and likely buyers in exchange for a profit
because unless you can sell, your business will
go to hell and you will find yourself living in a
van down by the river.*

"MOST ENTREPRENEURS ARE MERELY TECHNICIANS WITH AN ENTREPRENEURIAL SEIZURE. MOST ENTREPRENEURS FAIL BECAUSE THEY ARE WORKING IN THEIR BUSINESS RATHER THAN ON THEIR BUSINESS."
- MICHAEL GERBER

(Thrivetime Show Podcast guest and the best-selling author of the *E-MYTH REVISITED*.)

Once upon a time, when I started DJconnection.com my "normal" day looked like this:

- *3:00 am- Wakeup*

- *3:30 am- Lift Weights*

- *4:30 am- Get Ready*

- *5:00 am- Organize My Day*

- *7:00 am- Work On System Enhancement*

- *8:00 am-12:00 pm-*
  Make Dream 100 Calls

- *12:00 pm- 6:00 pm- Call Sales Leads And Do Sales/*
  Meetings With Brides

- *6:00 pm - 7:00 pm- Train disc jockeys before I could*
  afford to be full-time Self-employed, I worked at
  Applebee's, Target, and DirecTV. That way, I could save up
  the Money Needed To Build DJconnection.com

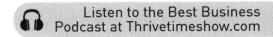

DAY 6

WAKE UP TWO HOURS BEFORE YOU SEE ANOTHER HUMAN

. . . .

If you are going to build an organization you must be organized. Think about that for a second. You can't be looking overwhelmed, disorganized, and perpetually distracted. If you are going to build an organization you must be organized, and you must create the plan and then get your employees to implement the plan. No hard-working ambitious person will work for a leader who is constantly disorganized and operating from reactive and emotional states that broadcasts to the world that they are overwhelmed.

Thus, you must wake up two hours before you see another human. Today, my alarm went off at 3 AM. Why? Because I want to get up and organize my day before other humans, partners, employees, clients, podcast guests, event organizers, influencers, authors, and the rest of humanity begins to bombard me with questions that are often both urgent and emotional.

NOTABLE QUOTABLE

"People around you, constantly under the pull of their emotions, change their ideas by the day or by the hour, depending on their mood. You must never assume that what people say or do in a particular moment is a statement of their permanent desires."

» **ROBERT GREENE**

(A guest on the Thrivetime Show podcast, an iconic author on strategy and power. When reading Robert Greene's books it is important to know that people that do not read the Bible and who do not adhere to God's laws often use *The 48 Laws of Power* against you in a nefarious way. I believe that it's important to know the moves that nefarious people will use against you so that you can protect yourself against the evil moves and the problems they will cause you. He has written seven international bestsellers, including *The 48 Laws of Power*, *The Art of Seduction*, *The 33 Strategies of War*, *The 50th Law* (with rapper 50 Cent), *Mastery*, *The Laws of Human Nature*, and *The Daily Laws*.)

So what time do I go to bed? Good question. I like to go to bed 6 hours before I wake up. However, you need to figure out what time you need to go to sleep in order to become a proactive and productive leader that is both organized and energetic. I personally go to bed at 9 PM and I wake up at 3 AM. However, YOU must design the schedule that works best for you starting now. Personally, I enjoy scheduling every minute of every day and I find unscheduled time to be depressing.

NOTABLE QUOTABLE

"Self-discipline begins with the mastery of your thoughts. If you don't control what you think, you can't control what you do. Simply, self-discipline enables you to think first and act afterward."

» **NAPOLEON HILL**

(The legendary author of *Think & Grow Rich* and the best-selling self-help author of his lifetime. Napoleon Hill's book *Think & Grow Rich* changed my life, so I named my son Aubrey Napoleon-Hill Clark and I don't regret it at all.)

"EVERYDAY, WAKE UP BEFORE EVERYONE ELSE IN YOUR HOME DOES."
– CLAY CLARK
(Founder of ThriveTimeShow.com, former U.S. SBA Entrepreneur of the Year, host of the ThriveTime Show, and America's #1 Business Coach.)

The F7 Life
DESIGN THE LIFE YOU WANT OR LIVE THE LIFE YOU DON'T WANT BY DEFAULT.

Psalm 118:24

"This is the day that the Lord has made. We will rejoice and be glad in it."

F7

What are Your F7 Goals?

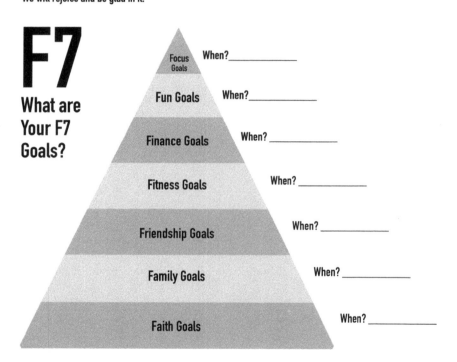

Focus Goals — When?_____

Fun Goals — When?_____

Finance Goals — When?_____

Fitness Goals — When?_____

Friendship Goals — When?_____

Family Goals — When?_____

Faith Goals — When?_____

Note: The shape of this time management has NO relation to the Egyptians, the Illuminati, Free Masons, or some multi-level pyramid scheme.

"Control your destiny or someone else will."

JACK WELCH
Former CEO of GE who grew the company by 4,000% during his tenure as CEW

What is your biggest limiting factor?

What questions do you have?

What do you do when you organize your day? Great question, I'm glad you asked. Write out your daily goals for your faith, family, finances, fitness, friendship, and fun. What are today's goals for the following areas of your life and when will you block out time to work on these goals?

FAITH GOALS:

What are your goals?

_____
_____

At what specific time will you work on these goals?

_____

FAMILY GOALS

What are your goals?

_____
_____

At what specific time will you work on these goals?

_____

FINANCIAL GOALS

What are your goals?

_____
_____

At what specific time will you work on these goals?

FITNESS GOALS

What are your goals?

_____

_____

At what specific time will you
work on these goals?

_____

FRIENDSHIP GOALS

What are your goals?

_____

_____

At what specific time will you
work on these goals?

_____

FUN GOALS

What are your goals?

_____

_____

At what specific time will you
work on these goals?

_____

NOTABLE QUOTABLE

"Thinking is the hardest work there is, which is probably the reason why so few engage in it."

» HENRY FORD

(The founder of Ford Motor Company. Ford was born in a farmhouse in Michigan's Springwells Township, leaving home at age 16 to find work in Detroit. It was a few years before this time that Ford first experienced automobiles, and throughout the later half of the 1880s, Ford began repairing and later constructing engines, and through the 1890s worked with a division of Edison Electric. He officially founded the Ford Motor Company in 1903 (at the age of 40), after prior failures in business but success in constructing automobiles. Remember Henry Ford founded Ford at the age of 40 after prior failure in business.)

Once you have taken the time needed to think about the goals related to your day, you must create a to-do list for your day and you must block out time in your calendar for each and every day. Do this process every single day until you are SUPER SUCCESSFUL. If you want to be half-ass, then your whole life will be terrible. But if you want your life to be abundant and successful, you must organize your day each and every day to build a thriving organization. Remember, what gets scheduled gets done. You must block out time every single day to create a clear picture of what your SUPER SUCCESSFUL and PRODUCTIVE DAY will look like.

"Idle hands are the devil's workshop."

» PROVERBS 16:27

LEARN HOW TO START AND GROW A BUSINESS BY LISTENING TO THE THRIVETIMESHOW.COM PODCAST TODAY!

61

NOTABLE QUOTABLE

"With no clear picture of how you wish your life to be, how on earth are you going to live it? What is your Primary Aim? Where is the script to make your dreams come true? What is the first step to take and how do you measure your progress? How far have you gone and how close are you to getting to your goals?"

» **MICHAEL GERBER**

(*Thrivetime Show Podcast* guest and the best-selling author of the *E-Myth Revisited*.)

Now back to the Carnivore Diet. I'm currently trying to get Doctor Shawn Baker to speak at our next business workshop and I am only eating meat. I'm down 5 pounds so far and I am feeling good. The biggest issue is focusing on and making sure I am only eating meat, which means not eating other things. Now that I am focused on eating meat, it is becoming clear how much of eating is simply a social activity or something that is done during social settings to fill the time. I'm eating ice chips and drinking more and more water. Being intentional and focusing on only eating meat is the key. Whether it is a diet or growing a business, simplicity scales and complexity fails.

NOTABLE QUOTABLE

"Your mindset is like a muscle. The more you exercise it, the stronger it gets."

» **DOCTOR SHAWN BAKER**

(Best-selling author of *The Carnivore Diet* and legendary Joe Rogan Podcast guest.)

Much like choosing to get up 2 hours before you see another human every day, choosing to eat only meat might not be the most fun thing in the world, but it is effective. Knowing there are simply 4 steps to successfully implementing the EXTREME and proven path to successful weight loss on the Carnivore Diet is mind-freeing and profoundly humbling. Knowing that I know exactly what to eat to reach my desired results is accountability-causing.

STEP 1 -
Only eat meat.

STEP 2 -
Only drink coffee or water.

STEP 3 -
Don't eat anything other than meat.

STEP 4 -
Don't drink anything other than coffee or water.

Quick Note:

Perhaps, I've mentioned this in the past, but very close to now, you are going to have to sell a solution to your ideal and likely buyers in exchange for a profit because unless you can sell, your business will go to hell.

"EVERYONE HERE HAS THE SENSE THAT RIGHT
NOW IS ONE OF THOSE MOMENTS WHEN WE ARE
INFLUENCING THE FUTURE."
–STEVE JOBS

(The co-founder of Apple, the founder of NeXT, and the former CEO of
PIXAR. Steve Jobs is the man who introduced the following technology
revolutions to the world: personal computing to the world, modern
computer animated movies, downloadable music, the iPhone (SMART phone),
the iPad, the iPod, etc.)

FOR BOTH EDUCATIONAL AND CATHARTIC REASONS I HAVE LISTED OUT JUST A FEW OF THE WAYS I HAVE BEEN SCREWED BY PARTNERS IN THE PAST:

» A partner embezzled money to fund the dating of an employee.

» A partner consistently lied about the commissions I was owed.

» A partner cheated on their spouse while dating an employee.

» A partner plotted to push me out of their company simply to increase their profits.

» A partner attempted to hire my employees away to start their own business, to compete with me.

» A partner consistently missed their meetings, did not do their job, and stole money.

FUN FACT: CLAY CLARK'S THRIVETIMESHOW PODCAST
HAS HIT #1 ON THE ITUNES PODCAST CHART SIX TIMES

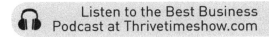

DAY 7

DO NOT PARTNER WITH MOST PEOPLE

· ·

You should not partner with most people. In fact it is probably best for your relationships with most people that you do not partner with most people. I would not partner with someone just because you are related to them or just because you are married to them. GET SERIOUS ABOUT THIS!!!

NOTABLE QUOTABLE

"Face reality as it is, not as it was or as you wish it to be."

» **JACK WELCH**

(The former CEO of GE who grew the company by 4,000% during his tenure as the CEO of GE.)

I find that many businesses struggle to have success because they simply have employees or business partners that refuse to work and this is not shocking to me.

FUN FACT

....

"85% of job applicants lie on resumes."

- Inc. Magazine

https://www.inc.com/jt-odonnell/staggering-85-of-job-applicants-lying-on-resumes-.html

FUN FACT

....

"78% of the men interviewed had cheated on their current partner."
– 5 Myths About Cheating

https://www.washingtonpost.com/opinions/five-myths-about-cheating/2012/02/08/gIQANGdaBR_story.html?noredirect=on&utm_term=.05ab54a87466

FUN FACT

....

"75% of employees steal from the workplace and most do so repeatedly."

https://www.cbsnews.com/news/employee-theft-are-you-blind-to-it/

FACT:

....

"American adults spend over 11 hours per day interacting with the media."

https://www.ThrivetimeShow.com/business-podcasts/sex-drugs-and-scams-business-coach-diaries/

When I was 16 years old and building my first successful business, DJConnection.com, I did not understand this. I thought naively at the time, that most people wanted to be successful most of the time and thus, I could simply hire friends to help me. At first, all of my friends liked the idea of working with or for me because they knew that I was making great money. However, once I started to hold my friends accountable for being on time, delivering a great entertainment experience and following the checklists and systems that I had built, my friends became less friendly. Soon, my friends were no longer my friends and I found myself without employees and without friends. Quickly, I began to understand that you want to hire A-Players to work for you.

Regardless of whether they are friends of yours or not. What's an A-Player? A-Players show up to work early, they don't leave until the job is done, they have great energy, and they are very coachable. When you work with family and friends, they are almost always completely uncoachable because they are your friend. When you start working with your spouse, NOW YOUR LIFE WILL GET CRAZY UP IN YOUR HOUSE!!! Don't do that to yourself!

NOTABLE QUOTABLE

"Every time I read a management or self-help book, I find myself saying, "That's fine, but that wasn't really the hard thing about the situation." The hard thing isn't setting a big, hairy, audacious goal. The hard thing is laying people off when you miss the big goal. The hard thing isn't hiring great people. The hard thing is when those "great people" develop a sense of entitlement and start demanding unreasonable things. The hard thing isn't setting up an organizational chart. The hard thing is getting people to communicate within the organization that you just designed. The hard thing isn't dreaming big. The hard thing is waking up in the middle of the night in a cold sweat when the dream turns into a nightmare."

» **BEN HOROWITZ**

(The billionaire entrepreneur, best-selling author, and the founder of Opsware, which was sold to Hewlett-Packard in 2007. Ben's book, *The Hard Thing About Hard Things: Building a Business When There Are No Easy Answers* is a tremendous book for entrepreneurs who are struggling to manage people and to grow a business. However, I would recommend reading Jack Welch's *Winning* if you are truly looking for the best book ever written on management.)

Don't force your spouse to work with you if your spouse is not an A-Player in the workplace, or you will begin to hate the very sight of their face and this is not good.

As an employer, you must face reality and the reality is that you are going to employ REAL people on the REAL planet Earth, and you are going to quickly become an expert of dealing with the moral depravity facing our society while trying to run a profitable business. I've been self-employed since I was 16 years old, thus, as of the time I am writing this, I've been employed for 27 years. Why am I telling you this? I'm telling you this because you are about ready to face a buffet of facts related to the moral decay of America. The facts below are why I unapologetically tell entrepreneurs to not partner with most people.

Do you remember when childhood was supposed to be about exploration, love, and innocence? They don't.

- A study put together in 2006 by the Centers for Disease Control and Prevention showed that 1 in 4 women and 1 in 6 men were sexually abused before the age of 18. This means there are more than 42 million adult survivors of child sexual abuse in the United States.

Did your father ever tell you what it meant to be a man or a woman? Their fathers didn't.

- According to research conducted by the *U.S. Census Bureau* and posted on Fatherhood.org, nearly 24 million children in America (1 out of 3) live in homes where the biological father is absent..

- According to a study done by the Fulton County Texas Department of Corrections, 85% of all youths in prison come from fatherless homes. Thus, kids who come from fatherless homes are nearly 20 times more likely to go to jail than kids who were raised in a home with their biological fathers.

- According to a September 1988 study by the United States Department of Justice, 70% of youths in state-operated institutions come from fatherless homes – 9 times the average.

Did you ever get in trouble with your parents for not studying hard and doing well on your tests? They never did.

- In a 2011 article written by Lory Hough, the *Harvard School of Education* found that over 50% of the 18-24 year old Americans surveyed by *National Geographic* couldn't find the state of New York on a map.

- In a Sept 14, 2011 article posted by Michael Winter for *USA Today*, the College Board now shows that just 40% of the high school seniors met benchmarks for college success.

Did your parents ever teach you about the consequences of your actions? Their parents never did.

- In a May of 2008 article published in *USA Today*, researchers in Chicago found that 1 in 4 teen girls have a sexually transmitted disease. Thus, approximately 3 million teens now have an STD.

- In a March 9th, 2012 article posted on *Reuters* by JoAnne Allen, about 16% of Americans between the ages of 14 and 49 are infected with genital herpes, making it one of the most common sexually transmitted diseases.

- In *Newsweek's* cover story entitled "iCrazy", it was revealed that one quarter of employees who use the internet during work visit porn sites. In fact, hits to porn sites are highest during office hours than at any other time of day.

Did your parents tell you not to lie? Their parents never did.

- 40% of the information on résumés is misrepresented (false, untrue, a lie) according to research conducted by *American DataBank* from 2008 - 2010.

Did your parents ever teach you that a quitter never wins and that a winner never quits? Their parents never did.

- Despite being in a deep economic recession, a July 7th, 2010 article published by the *Harvard Business Review* reported that more employees quit their jobs than were terminated, according to the *US Bureau of Labor Statistics* 3 month research.

Do you remember when college was supposed to make you more intelligent and more hireable? They don't.

- According to a *USA Today* Article written by Mary Beth Marklein, research shows students spent 50% less time studying compared with students a few decades ago. The research compared college students enrolled in 2001 versus college students enrolled in 2011.

Whatever happened to common sense?

- According to Gail Cunningham, In a 2011 *Newsweek* Article, research was conducted by asking 1,000 U.S. citizens to take America's official citizenship test. 29% couldn't name the Vice President. Spokeswoman for the National Foundation of Credit Counseling, as quoted in a July 2012 article in *Newsweek Magazine*, 56% of U.S. adults admit they don't have a budget; one-third don't pay all their bills on time.

"Nothing will work unless you do."

» **MAYA ANGELOU**
(Poet, producer, actress and prolific writer.)

- According to an article written by Mary Beth Marklein in *USA Today*, nearly half of the nation's undergraduates show almost no gains in learning in their first two years of college. The report concludes this is because, in large part, colleges don't make academics a priority. Among their top activities, students report spending 24% of their time sleeping, 51% of their time socializing and just 7% actually studying.

If you work hard and commit yourself to excellence, anyone can obtain the American dream. But what if you don't want to work hard?

- In a study published in *Inc. Magazine* in June of 2007 and written by Liz Webber, research showed that average employees wasted an average of 1.7 hours of an 8.5 hour workday, while 20-29 year olds wasted 2.1 hours per day.

- A Leadership IQ study of 6,000 workers featured on *Fox News* in 2008, revealed that in 2008 nearly 25% of the average American's workday was wasted. Thus, the average employee was reported to waste nearly 2.3 hours per day.

- In a February 22, 2010 article featured in *Inc. Magazine* and written by Kim Boatman, research conducted by SpectorSoft Corp, concluded that 89% of the businesses that were studied discovered employees were wasting time or abusing Internet use.

- In an article posted on Salary.com by Aaron Goveia in 2012, a study showed almost two-thirds of employees admitted to wasting time at work on the computer each day. The next obvious question is, how much time?

Do you remember what it was like to converse with someone who wasn't updating their Facebook status and texting while waiting for you to finish speaking? They don't.

- According to research conducted by *Research Basex* and reported in a February issue of *USA Today*, "productivity losses due to the cost of unnecessary interruptions" were at $650 billion in 2007.

- In a 2002 article published by *New York Times* Best-Selling Author Ken Blanchard, a large survey of 1,300 private-sector companies, conducted by Proudfoot Consulting, found that on average only 59% of work time is productive.

- A March 2, 2011 study published by *Inc. Magazine* shows employees are unproductive for half of the day.

- In an article posted by Martha C. White on March 13th, 2012 entitled, *"You're Wasting Time at Work Right Now, Aren't You?"* revealed that a 2012 study of 3,200 employees conducted by Salary.com showed that 64% say they visit websites unrelated to work daily.

Do you remember when 1 out of 5 of your co-workers wasn't insane? They don't.

- According to a disturbing article published by *Harvard Health Publications* in February of 2010, researchers analyzing results from the *U.S. National Co-morbidity* Survey found a nationally representative study of Americans ages 15 to 54. In that study, it was reported that 18% of those who were employed said they experienced symptoms of a mental health disorder in the previous month.

Don't Partner with Dumb People

"Whenever I watch TV and see those poor starving kids all over the world, I can't help but cry. I mean I'd love to be skinny like that but not with all those flies and death and stuff."

» **MARIAH CAREY, POP SINGER**

Consider this: Research reported in the *New York Times* reports that currently 45% of people who have attended college for two years are for the first time showing no improvements in their cognitive or critical thinking skills.

At the middle school and high school level, kids are supposed to learn how to learn. As more and more technology is introduced into the classroom, less and less teaching is done. Teachers

 VERIFY THIS INSANITY AT:

http://opinionator.blogs.nytimes.com/2011/09/21/what-do-test-scores-tell-us/

are simply clicking through an endless series of multimedia presentations on their "fancy" technology presentation boards while students are listening to Lil' Wayne on their iPhones. The teacher's job of instructing, challenging, and inspiring students has now been replaced with their new job of babysitting, breaking up fights, taking attendance, and managing the kids in a "politically correct way." Large numbers of teachers I've spoken to have told me that they spend well over half of their time dealing with behavior problems, and what's left of their time is now spent teaching the students anything.

Don't Partner with Perpetually Distracted People

Distracted Driving Kills People, Distracted Workers Kill Your Bottom Line

We all know that research clearly shows that distracted driving kills people. It's a little tough to focus on driving while sending an intense text to your ex or to turn while attempting to learn what happened at yesterday's meeting via text. We all know how frustrating it can be to watch a movie with someone who won't quit asking questions while the film is showing, or how maddening it can be to golf with someone who keeps taking cell phone calls while you're attempting to putt.

However, businesses throughout the country are paying employees who are completely mentally disengaged from the workplace. Joe is texting Sally about dinner plans, the upcoming game, and home drama on your time and all of the time. Countless research is now revealing that between non-work related emails and texts, smoke breaks, and social media, video games, nearly 40% of the average employee's workday is spent doing something other than working. And again, nearly half of those people are already struggling with being dumb and dishonest.

FUN FACT: CLAY CLARK'S THRIVETIMESHOW PODCAST HAS HIT #1 ON THE ITUNES PODCAST CHART SIX TIMES

VERIFY THIS INSANITY AT:

http://www.usatoday.com/tech/columnist/kimkomando/story/2012-02-24/
work-monitor-smartphone/53221804/1

Although the information above makes me want to staple my forehead out of frustration, I am sincerely encouraged by your ability to break out of the clutter of commerce. This can be accomplished if you will simply devote yourself to studying successful companies and doing what they have done to build their billion-dollar brands. However, because I know you are too busy to devote ten years of your life to reading case studies to develop the action plans as I have done, the rest of this book is dedicated to providing you with the proven and practical plans used by America's biggest and most loved brands. In this uncertain economic environment brands including Disney, QuikTrip, Chick-Fil-A, Southwest Airlines, Apple, and other companies are still producing BIG RESULTS by implementing these plans; and now you can too!

Don't Partner with Dishonest People

Will Your Stuff Still Be There When Your Employee
Goes Home For the Night?

Assuming that you have found an employee that doesn't have a coy fish tattoo on their neck and that shows up on time, you still wouldn't be in the clear yet; unless you are okay with them stealing all of your profits. According to a study conducted by the U.S. Chamber of Commerce and published in *Inc. Magazine*, one-third of all business bankruptcies are a result of theft in the workplace. This is insane to me. Shouldn't this be talked about? To me, one-third is an absurdly large percentage. Wow! Please excuse me as I deal with my nausea.

 VERIFY THIS INSANITY AT:

http://www.inc.com/articles/1999/05/13731.html

"FACE REALITY AS IT IS, NOT AS IT WAS
OR AS YOU WISH IT TO BE."
– JACK WELCH
FORMER CEO OF GENERAL ELECTRIC
Who grew the company by 4,000 % during g his time as CEO

NOTABLE QUOTABLES

"The most important decisions you make are not the things you do, but the things you decide not to do."

» STEVE JOBS

(The co-founder of Apple, the founder of NeXT, and the former CEO of PIXAR. Steve Jobs is the man who introduced the following technology revolutions to the world: personal computing to the world, modern computer animated movies, downloadable music, the iPhone (SMART phone), the iPad, the iPod, etc.)

"As we became leaner, we found ourselves communicating better, with fewer interpreters and fewer filters. We found that with fewer layers we had wider spans of management. We weren't managing better. We were managing less, and that was better."

» JACK WELCH

(Iconic former CEO of GE who grew GE by 4,000% during his tenure. Jack Welch is the best-selling author of *Straight from the Gut* & *Winning*, which is the best management book ever written.)

"People who are unable to get things done must be fired. At Trump our value is based upon the "You can make excuses or you can make money"

» DONALD TRUMP

(Real Estate Mogul, Author, and the man behind the TRUMP brands.)

NOTABLE QUOTABLE

"If you aren't fired up with enthusiasm, you'll be fired with enthusiasm."

» **VINCE LOMBARDI**

(Legendary National Football League Hall of Fame coach. He is best known as the head coach of the Green Bay Packers during the 1960s, where he led the team to three straight, and five total NFL Championships in seven years, in addition to winning the first two Super Bowls at the conclusion of the 1966 and 1967 NFL seasons.)

"Lazy hands make a man poor, but diligent hands bring wealth."

» **PROVERBS 10:4**

(The Bible has an incredible author, God. The book proverbs is a book that is proverbs. The book is in favor of action. If you are looking for a book that is focused on the action steps that you need to take in order to achieve success on the planet Earth from a Christian perspective, read Proverbs.)

Now back to eating only meat and the Carnivore Diet. The Carnivore diet works because it is simple and doable. It does not require much thought and that is how a scalable business should run. You want to build your business to be so simple that a complete idiot can be successful while working in your business. Every day, I wake up thinking about eating meat and then I go to bed thinking about eating meat. When it's time to eat, I think about meat. What can I eat? Only meat. Whether it is a diet or growing a business, simplicity scales and complexity fails.

NOTABLE QUOTABLE

....

"While the carnivore diet is increasingly becoming popular, I still get people asking me if vegetables are part of the diet! Looks like I still have a lot of work to do to get the message out!!"

» **DOCTOR SHAWN BAKER**

(Best-selling author of *The Carnivore Diet* and legendary Joe Rogan Podcast guest.)

Much like choosing to get up 2 hours before you see another human every day, choosing to eat only meat might not be the most fun thing in the world, but it is effective. Knowing there are simply 4 steps to successfully implementing the EXTREME and proven path to successful weight loss on the Carnivore Diet is mind-freeing and challenging because it requires extreme accountability to implement a proven plan.

STEP 1 -
Only eat meat.

STEP 2 -
Only drink coffee or water.

STEP 3 -
Don't eat anything other than meat.

STEP 4 -
Don't drink anything other than coffee or water.

Quick Note:

Always keep in mind that soon and very soon you are going to have to sell a solution to your ideal and likely buyers in exchange for a profit because unless you can sell, your business will go to hell. Unless you aspire to live in perpetual poverty you must soon learn to sell something.

NOTABLE QUOTABLE

"My son is now an entrepreneur. That is what you are called when you didn't have a job."

» **TED TURNER**

(The founder of TBS, TNT, CNN, and the former owner of the Atlanta Braves and Atlanta Hawks.)

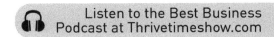
DAY 8

CONVERT YOUR DRIVE TIME INTO YOUR SELF-HELP LEARNING TIME

. . . .

You and I all have just 24 hours in each day. However, if you spend time studying super successful people you will quickly notice that super successful people are masters of time management. They don't waste time engaged in mindless activities that are not related to the achievement of the goals they have for their faith, family, finances, fitness, friendship, and fun.

Thus, YOU must also become a master of time management. And thus, to help you to become a master of time management, I am going to teach you 10 quick super moves you must use to become a time management expert, guru and master.

PRO-TIP #1 - Block out time in your schedule for what matters. Today, I am writing this chapter of the book before most people are even awake. Why? Because I blocked out time to write this chapter of the book. Is anyone telling me to write this chapter of the book today? Is there a boss following up with me about writing this book? No. So why am I writing this chapter of this book? I am writing this chapter of the book because I BELIEVE IN YOU, and I chose to block out time to write this chapter of this book on this very day.

NOTABLE QUOTABLE

"Management is doing things right; leadership is doing the right things."

» **PETER DRUCKER**

(The legendary management consultant educator, and author, whose writings contributed to the philosophical and practical foundations of modern management theory. He was also a leader in the development of management education, and invented the concepts known as management by objectives and self-control, and he has been described as "the founder of modern management".)

I find that many businesses struggle to have success because they simply have employees or business partners that refuse to work and this is not shocking to me.

PRO-TIP #2 - Avoid spending time with negative people that do not understand how to become a successful entrepreneur. Negative people are like cancerous growth and people that do not know how to become successful, will constantly bombard you with their bad ideas and their bad advice. When possible, choose to spend time with successful people that are going places with their life. You will

FUN FACT: CLAY CLARK'S THRIVETIMESHOW PODCAST HAS HIT #1 ON THE ITUNES PODCAST CHART SIX TIMES

become the average of the five people you spend the most time with whether they are positive or negative. Block out time in your schedule to be around super successful people. If super successful people don't want to spend time with you, offer to intern for FREE or to work in their office for FREE. Find a way to be in the room with super successful people.

NOTABLE QUOTABLE

"No one lives long enough to learn everything they need to learn starting from scratch. To be successful, we absolutely, positively have to find people who have already paid the price to learn the things that we need to learn to achieve our goals."

» **BRIAN TRACY**

(The legendary best-selling author, sales trainer, business growth consultant, and keynote success speaker.)

PRO-TIP #3 - Use social media, the internet, and your computer as a tool and don't allow yourself to become a tool. Be very intentional when you will use your computer and when you will not. Don't allow the internet or your computer to consume your day with mindless clicking, scrolling and screen time that is not related to achieving success.

"American adults spend over 11 hours per day listening to, watching, reading or generally interacting with the media."
— *Time Flies: U.S. Adults Now Spend Nearly Half a Day Interacting with Media*

READ - https://www.nielsen.com/insights/2018/time-flies-us-adults-now-spend-nearly-half-a-day-interacting-with-media/

PRO-TIP #4 - Always work via appointment. When possible schedule appointments with people as opposed to playing endless phone tag with humanity all day every day. When possible, schedule a specific time to talk to people and make these interactions as meaningful and short as possible.

PRO-TIP #5 - Refuse to engage in small talk and gossip. Small talk leads to the non-achievement of even small goals. Go out of your way to not participate in gossip filled conversation not related to the achievement of a goal. Run away from emotional conversations filled with urgent emotional arguments, feelings and opinions. Choose to only engage in conversations related to the achievement of big goals when possible.

NOTABLE QUOTABLE

....

"27 Idle hands are the devil's workshop; idle lips are his mouthpiece. 28 An evil man sows strife; gossip separates the best of friends. 29 Wickedness loves company—and leads others into sin."

» **PROVERBS 16: 27-19**

PRO-TIP #6 - Don't go out to dinner and lunch with people unless it's related to the achievement of your goals. I see so many entrepreneurs who tell me they don't have time to achieve their goals, yet spend massive quantities of time going out to dinner with people to engage in small talk. When possible, eat quickly and get back to the achievement of your goals.

PRO-TIP #7 - Don't watch TV or movies that are not related to the achievement of your goals. Instead of watching movies about other people, why don't you live a life that people would want to make a movie about.

PRO-TIP #8 - Spend more time planning your life than planning your next vacation. Design your days and life in a way where you love each day so much that you sincerely don't want to escape your daily schedule to go on vacation.

NOTABLE QUOTABLE

"With no clear picture of how you wish your life to be, how on earth are you going to live it? What is your Primary Aim? Where is the script to make your dreams come true? What is the first step to take and how do you measure your progress? How far have you gone and how close are you to getting to your goals?"

» **MICHAEL GERBER**

(Thrivetime Show Podcast guest and the best-selling author of the *E-Myth Revisited*.)

PRO-TIP #9 - You must carry a to-do list at all times. You must always write down the tasks and actions items you need to be working on so that you don't drift throughout the day without purpose and without focus during each and every minute of your day. If you have a "BIG IDEA" write it down. If you have a small item that you don't want to forget, write it down. If you are making a shopping list in your mind, write it down. If you think of something important, write it down. The pen is for remembering and the mind is for thinking.

NOTABLE QUOTABLE

....

"Mastery is not about being special or more gifted than anyone else. Mastery is a direct result of pigheaded discipline and determination."

» **CHET HOLMES**

(The legendary business consultant, business growth coach, and the best-selling author of *The Ultimate Sales Machine*.)

PRO-TIP #10 - Block time to schedule and plan your day and you must carry a calendar with your schedule at all times. What gets scheduled gets done. Stop forgetting appointments. Stop double booking yourself for things and stop running out of time to get things done and start using a calendar at all times. I have never met a SUPER SUCCESSFUL PERSON that does not use a calendar and to-do list at all times.

NOTABLE QUOTABLE

....

"The secret of your success is largely determined by your daily agenda."

» **JOHN MAXWELL**

(Thrivetime Show guest and the best-selling author of *The 21 Irrefutable Laws of Leadership*.)

Speaking of eating only meat and the Carnivore Diet. The Carnivore diet works, but only if I only eat meat. Every day, I wake up thinking about eating meat and then I go to bed thinking about eating meat, because that is the only food that I am allowing myself to eat. When it's time to eat, I only eat meat. What can I eat? Only meat. Whether it is a diet or growing a business, simplicity scales and complexity fails.

NOTABLE QUOTABLE

....

"The only limit to your potential is the mindset you choose to adopt."

» **DOCTOR SHAWN BAKER**

(Best-selling author of *The Carnivore Diet* and legendary Joe Rogan Podcast guest)

"ONE OF THE PENALTIES OF LEADERSHIP IS THE NECESSITY OF WILLINGNESS UPON THE PART OF THE LEADER TO DO MORE THAN HE REQUIRES OF HIS FOLLOWERS."
- NAPOLEON HILL

(The best-selling author of Think and Grow Rich. The man who I named my son after because Think and Grow Rich changed my life.)

Much like choosing to become a master of time management, choosing to eat only meat might not be the most fun thing in the world, but it works!!! Knowing there are simply 4 steps to successfully implementing the EXTREME and proven path to successful weight loss on the Carnivore Diet is mind-freeing and incredible!!!

STEP 1 -
Only eat meat.

STEP 2 -
Only drink coffee or water.

STEP 3 -
Don't eat anything other than meat.

STEP 4 -
Don't drink anything other than coffee or water.

Quick Note:

I'm not sure if this is a good time to talk about it or not, but SOON and VERY, VERY close to now, you are going to have to sell a solution to your ideal and likely buyers in exchange for a profit. Unless you can sell, your business will go to hell and you will run out of money which is typically not viewed as good, ideal, or funny.

"ENTREPRENEURS SOLVE THE WORLD'S PROBLEMS
AND UNAPOLOGETICALLY MAKE MONEY DOING IT."
– CLAY CLARK

(Founder of ThriveTimeShow.com, former U.S. SBA
Entrepreneur of the Year, host of the ThriveTime Show,
and America's #1 Business Coach.)

FUN FACT: CLAY CLARK'S THRIVETIMESHOW PODCAST
HAS HIT #1 ON THE ITUNES PODCAST CHART SIX TIMES

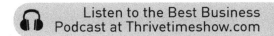

DAY 9

ESTABLISH SEPARATE CREDIT CARDS FOR BUSINESS & PERSONAL SPENDING

· · · · · · · · · ·

Alright, we are on day 9 together and we have reached a turning point! It's now time to get really practical and tactical. From this point forward everything I will teach you is going to be very specific, linear and action-oriented to the max!

You must go to www.CreditCards.com and apply to obtain three separate credit cards.

1. Apply for a **personal** credit card.

2. Apply for a **business** credit card.

3. Apply for a **second business** card.

When your credit cards arrive in the mail, label the credit cards with masking tape what they are to be used for.

1. Only use your personal credit card for personal expenses.

2. Only use your business credit card for business expenses.

3. Only use your second business credit card for business expenses if your primary business card is not functioning properly.

By having clearly organized credit cards that you pay off each month in full, you will find it much easier to keep track of all of your expenses. Thus, when you are working with your accountants and bookkeepers they can make sure that your records are always updated and honest so that you never get in trouble with the Internal Revenue Service. It's very important that you keep your financial records honest and accurate.

Credit Card Pro-Tips:

Pay off your credit cards in full each month.

Never allow the business credit cards you share with your partners to finance the lavish lascivious dating of employees. Furthermore, never date employees. Furthermore, never sleep with employees. Furthermore, never sleep with employees and use the business credit card that you share with partners to finance your lascivious luxury dating of employees. I only write these practical tips because throughout the history of my life having worked with thousands of business owners, I have found many people tend to use their business credit cards in nefarious ways.

Speaking of only eating only meat and the Carnivore Diet. I have found that the most difficult thing about only eating meat is only eating meat. It's so simple, yet it is difficult to only eat meat when so much of the food available is not meat. In fact, it turns out that bread, vegetables, fruit, and ice cream are not meat.

NOTABLE QUOTABLE

"Nothing can stop the man with the right mental attitude from achieving his goal; nothing on earth can help the man with the wrong mental attitude."

» **THOMAS JEFFERSON**
(One of the Founding Fathers of the United States.)

Knowing there are simply 4 key steps to successfully implementing the EXTREME and proven path to successful weight loss on the Carnivore Diet is mind-freeing and incredible!!!

STEP 1 -
Only eat meat.

STEP 2 -
Only drink coffee or water.

STEP 3 -
Don't eat anything other than meat.

STEP 4 -
Don't drink anything other than coffee or water.

Quick Note:

I'm not sure if this is a good time to talk about it or not, but SOON and VERY, VERY close to now, you are going to have to sell a solution to your ideal and likely buyers in exchange for a profit because unless you can sell, your business will go to hell. I truly believe this is the moment of truth for an entrepreneur. If you cannot consistently sell your products at a profit to your ideal and likely buyers, you don't own a business, you are just involved in busyness.

"TEMPORARY FAILURES ARE A PREREQUISITE TO SUCCESS."
–NAPOLEON HILL

(A man who was mentored directly by the steel tycoon Andrew Carnegie, the best-selling self-help author of all-time during his lifetime, the author of *Think & Grow Rich*, *The Law of Success*, *The Master-Key to Riches*, etc...)

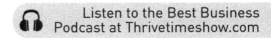

DAY 10

ESTABLISH YOUR REVENUE GOALS AND KNOCK OUT THESE ACTION ITEMS

. . . .

STEP 1 - Establishing Revenue Goals

Determine Your Annual Gross Revenue Goal:

_____

Determine Your Current Gross Revenue:

_____

Determine a Deadline and Date for the
Achievement of Your Gross Revenue Goal:

_____

BOOK YOUR TICKETS TO MY 2-DAY INTERACTIVE BUSINESS GROWTH WORKSHOP

https://www.ThrivetimeShow.com/conference/

We sell tickets for $250 or whatever price you can afford.

You can literally name your price. Why do I let wonderful people like you to name your price? I grew up poor and I know we all need a hand up from time to time. So find a way to go to navigate via the internet to www.ThrivetimeShow.com today and request a ticket for our next in-person 2-day interactive business growth workshop! I've been hosting workshops since 2005 and at the workshop we shall answer all of your business related questions, and shall teach you how to implement every concept found within this book.

Take Advantage of Your Ability to Ask Us (Clay Clark) Anything - Simply email over any business GROWTH related questions that you have to info@ThrivetimeShow.com and we shall turn your questions into a show. I'm not sure if you are aware of this or not, but 90% of the shows I record are based upon the questions that are submitted to me by our listeners. Over the past 10 years I've released 5,000+ shows including interviews with Wolfgang Puck, John Maxwell, professional sports stars, celebrity musicians, the founder of FUBU Daymon John, and countless super successful people including NBA Hall of Famer David Robinson, Michael Levine, Eric Trump, and more...

Determine in your mind RIGHT NOW to only feed your mind proven best-practice systems and success strategies. Simply refuse to listen to people that do not know what they are talking about. Over the years, Doctor Robert Zoellner and I have recorded the entire proven linear path to business success for you to listen to starting TODAY at: https://www.ThrivetimeShow.com/TowerOfPower

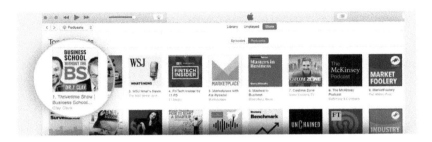

 Commit to saving time and money by not wasting your time and money in an attempt to reinvent the wheel. To make your life 2% better, I have documented and organized the proven processes, success strategies and turn-key business systems for you to use for FREE today at: https://www.ThrivetimeShow.com/Downloadables

NOTABLE QUOTABLE

"Whether you think you can, or you think you can't--you're right."

» **HENRY FORD**

(The man who transformed the automobile industry with his refinement of the assembly line system of manufacturing.)

LEARN HOW TO START AND GROW A BUSINESS BY LISTENING TO THE THRIVETIMESHOW.COM PODCAST TODAY!

97

ACTION ITEM

Listen to NBA Hall of Famer and ultra-successful venture capital investor David Robinson explaining the importance of bringing daily diligence and hard work everyday.

https://www. ThrivetimeShow.com/ business-podcasts/ importance-diligence- hard-work-nba- superstar-david- robinson/

When I first started DJConnection.com out of my parent's basement and then my college dorm room, I was obsessed with getting to $1,000,000 per year of sales. It was my magnificent white-hot obsession! I was obsessed about getting DJConnection.com to $1,000,000 in sales per year when I started the company out of my Oral Roberts University dorm room. I dreamed about it at night. I contemplated how to improve it while driving to Target to work. I made sales call for it while driving to job #2 working at Applebee's. While everyone was watching Survivor, the NFL, NBA, and ESPN's Sports Center, I was passing out fliers to promote the company because I knew I needed $19,230.77 per week to achieve my goal and $3,205.13 per day to turn my goal into reality.

NOTABLE QUOTABLE

"For years and years I [recorded my podcast] with no money in it forever. It took five years. It took a while. About five years later it started making money."

» **JOE ROGAN**

(Joe Rogan Experience Podcast #2,138 with Tucker Carlson.)

I'm sure that we have talked about it lately, but there are simply 4 steps to successfully implementing the EXTREME and the proven path to successful weight loss on the Carnivore Diet.

STEP 1 -
Only eat meat.

STEP 2 -
Only drink coffee or water.

STEP 3 -
Don't eat anything
other than meat.

STEP 4 -
Don't drink anything other than coffee or water.

NOTABLE QUOTABLE

"Character is like a tree and reputation
like a shadow. The shadow is what we
think of it; the tree is the real thing."

» **BENJAMIN FRANKLIN**

(An American polymath who was one of the Founding
Fathers of the United States. During his time,
Benjamin Franklin was a renowned author, politician,
scientist, inventor and diplomat. He alone convinced
the French to supply the United States with the
ammunition and weapons needed to win the war
against the British as the colonists faced certain
defeat without the French support.)

Quick Note:

I'm not sure if this is a good time to talk about it or not, but SOON and VERY, VERY close to now, you are going to have to sell a solution to your ideal and likely buyers in exchange for a profit because unless you can sell, your business will go to hell and you will fail. To run a successful business you must learn to sell or things will not go well.

NOTABLE QUOTABLE

"The main reason people struggling financially is because they have spent 8 years in school but learned nothing about money. The result is people learn to work for money, but never learn to have money work for them."

» **ROBERT KIYOSAKI**

(The best-selling author of *The Rich Dad Poor Dad* book series and a man who has sold over 40 million copies of his entrepreneur books.)

NOTABLE QUOTABLE

"The starting point of all achievement is DESIRE. Keep this constantly in mind. Weak desire brings weak results, just as a small fire makes a small amount of heat."

» **NAPOLEON HILL**

(A man who was mentored directly by the steel tycoon Andrew Carnegie, the best-selling self-help author of all-time during his lifetime, the author of *Think & Grow Rich, The Law of Success, The Master-Key to Riches*, etc...)

"*EVERYONE HERE HAS THE SENSE THAT RIGHT NOW IS ONE OF THOSE MOMENTS WHEN WE ARE INFLUENCING THE FUTURE.*"
–**STEVE JOBS**

(The co-founder of Apple, the founder of NeXT, and the former CEO of PIXAR. Steve Jobs is the man who introduced the following technology revolutions to the world: personal computing to the world, modern computer animated movies, downloadable music, the iPhone (SMART phone), the iPad, the iPod, etc.)

SUPER PLAYS

Determine how much money your business needs to produce per year just to break even:

_____

Break Even Formula:
Fixed Costs / Sales Price – Variable Costs = Break Even Point

Determine how much money your business needs to produce per month just to break even:

_____

Determine how much money your business needs to produce per week just to break even:

_____

FUN FACT: CLAY CLARK'S THRIVETIMESHOW PODCAST HAS HIT #1 ON THE ITUNES PODCAST CHART SIX TIMES

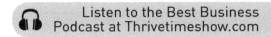

DAY 11

YOU MUST KNOW YOUR NUMBERS

. . . .

You must know your numbers. If you don't know your numbers you will soon discover that you are losing everything and you are en route to living in a van down by the river.

Determine the Number of Customers Per Month That You Need In Order to Achieve Your Goals:

Determine How Many Products and Services You Need to Sell Just to Break Even:

Determine the Number of Customers That You Need to Have to Break-Even Each Month:

Determine the Profit That You Will Make (On Average) Per Customer:

Determine the Total Gross Revenue Generated Per Deal:

**Determine Why You Decided
to Get Involved In the Business:**

Document How You Got Involved In the Business:

Back to the Elephant In The Room Story. My brother-in-law was living with us at the time and he really wanted to start a men's grooming business. However, despite knowing that he wanted to offer the men of Tulsa, a high-end men's grooming experience, he had no one willing to invest in him, no credit to speak of, and little to no money saved, no location to open the first store from, no knowledge of how to scale and grow a business. However, he did have access to me.

"I knew I wanted Clay Clark, my brother-in-law, to invest in me, and be my partner and mentor to grow my haircut business (Which Clay later decided to name Elephant In The Room Men's Grooming Lounge). At that time there was no name, it was just an idea in my head, a concept, a place men could go and relax, partake in an uplifting conversation while enjoying a tailored haircut. I want to point out that I was intentional on who I wanted to partner with, Clay was someone that had strengths in areas that may be my weak spots. Clay would bring the systems and marketing while

I would create the ground level experience and overall concept. It took me two years to earn Clay's respect and trust. I worked side by side with him. During this time of working with Clay, I saw him set his alarm at 4:00 AM every day. I saw him make his to-do-lists every day and I saw him put in the grind needed to create the success he achieved. After two years of getting up early, making to-do-lists, walking fast and working with him, I realized that he was a confident person because he made small daily commitments to himself and that he actually honored those commitments. Rather than feeling dissonance as a result of setting goals and not completing them, he actually was becoming a progressively more confident person every week I shadowed him. I started realizing that as a result of getting up at the same time as him, making my daily to-do-lists and living a purposeful life, I too was becoming a more confident person. Clay told me that he would match me dollar for dollar when it came to investing in the men's grooming business, and that he would provide the physical space for our first location. He told me he would supply the marketing, the systems, and he even supplied the name (Elephant In The Room Men's Grooming Lounge), the weekly coaching meetings, the website, the branding, the contacts and more.

An investment is as much in the people as it is the idea because when it comes down to it the people execute the idea making it reality. Clay and I worked side by side for the next 2 years, this time building my character, experience and Clay's trust in me as a partner so when it came time to put our money into our Men's Grooming Lounge he would be confident. During this process I had a lot of unanswered questions like, when would it be open, when would we find a location, I chose to focus and learn from all those experiences and that was ok that I didn't have the time or answers but more important I was growing everyday."

Justin Moore
*(Co-Founder of Elephant In
The Room Men's Grooming Lounge)*

Determine the repetitive daily action steps that you must take on a daily basis in order to turn your idea into a profitable business. As an example, with Elephant In The Room Men's Grooming Lounge, in order to grow the business we needed to do the following activities all day every day.

1st - We needed to write two fully optimized and keyword rich 1,000 word pages of original HTML (hypertext markup language) text and add it to the website every day. Why? Because getting to the top of the Google search results is critical marketing a men's grooming lounge business.

2nd - We needed to gather objective Google reviews from the real customers that we actually provided a real men's grooming service to. Why? Because most people on the planet earth use the Google search engine to find the products and services that they are looking for.

3rd - We needed to gather objective video reviews from the real customers that we actually provided a real men's grooming service to. Why? Because most humans on the planet will do a Google search for the name of the company and they will watch and or read objective reviews from real customers before deciding to do business with you.

4th - We needed to drop off FREE haircut cards to local businesses and invite them to check out our facility for a FREE complimentary first haircut. Why? Because there is a strong chance that nobody was waking up with a burning desire to pay us, especially if they didn't know we even existed.

5th - We had to post "now hiring" job posts and interview properly licensed stylists and men's grooming professionals every day. Why? Because once our ideal and likely buyers began to discover us, we needed to be able to cut their hair.

6th - We needed to put out our massive feather signs and election-sized street signs. Why? I call this concept "Signs and Wonders." You must put up physical signage that makes people wonder. What is that place? The sign says the first haircut is just a dollar. I wonder how that works?

 Listen to the following podcast to learn how to determine the profit per customer: https://www.thrivetimeshow.com/business-podcasts/determine-profit-per-customer-need-make/

It's been a minute and I don't know if I have brought it up enough lately, but there are simply 4 steps to successfully implementing the EXTREME and the proven path to successful weight loss on the Carnivore Diet.

NOTABLE QUOTABLE

"A goal is a dream with a deadline."

 » **NAPOLEON HILL**

(A man who was mentored directly by the steel tycoon Andrew Carnegie, the best-selling self-help author of all-time during his lifetime, the author of *Think & Grow Rich, The Law of Success, The Master-Key to Riches*, etc...)

FUN FACT: CLAY CLARK'S THRIVETIMESHOW PODCAST HAS HIT #1 ON THE ITUNES PODCAST CHART SIX TIMES

STEP 1 -
Only eat meat.

STEP 2 -
Only drink coffee or water.

STEP 3 -
Don't eat anything other than meat.

STEP 4 -
Don't drink anything other
than coffee or water.

Quick Note:

*"Do or do not,
there is no try."
- Yoda*
(The fictional green little man and
source of wisdom from the Star
Wars movie series)

LEARN HOW TO START AND GROW A BUSINESS BY LISTENING
TO THE THRIVETIMESHOW.COM PODCAST TODAY!

109

"*ENTREPRENEURS SOLVE THE WORLD'S PROBLEMS AND UNAPOLOGETICALLY MAKE MONEY DOING IT.*"
– CLAY CLARK

(Founder of ThriveTimeShow.com, former U.S. SBA
Entrepreneur of the Year, host of the ThriveTime Show,
and America's #1 Business Coach.)

FUN FACT:

Did you know that President Franklin Roosevelt and his lesbian wife introduced the concept of his socialist-inspired 40-hour work week in 1938?

Via the "Fair Labor Standards Act of 1938."

FUN FACT: CLAY CLARK'S THRIVETIMESHOW PODCAST
HAS HIT #1 ON THE ITUNES PODCAST CHART SIX TIMES

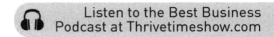

DAY 12

HOW MANY HOURS PER WEEK ARE YOU WILLING TO WORK IN YOUR BUSINESS

· · · · · · · · ·

Determine the number of hours you are willing to work in your business.

Don't make this a cognitive dissonance causing display of jack-assery (the cosmic default habit force that causes most people to become poor by default). By saying you are willing to work 80 hours per week. When in reality you are only willing to work 40 hours per week. Simply determine how many hours you are willing to work and stick to it. I like to go to bed at 9:00 PM and wake up at 3:00 AM. That is what I like to do. Now I'm asking you.

- What time will you intentionally choose to go to bed each night?

- What time will you choose to wake up each morning?

Create a calendar and block out the times that you are willing to work on your business.

Create a to-do list every day filled with the action steps that you will actually complete each day. Do not make to-do lists that you will never complete. Do not create to-do lists filled with vague wishes.

Keep your to-do list with you at all times. Never forget important details, by never attempting to remember them. Write down details, take notes and write down anything that you must do throughout your day on your to-do list.

But what about life-balance?

I only bring this up because 100% of clients ask me this question. However, the answer is very simple. What gets scheduled gets done and what does not get scheduled will not get done. I am writing this book right now during the time that I have blocked out for writing this book. I am not shocked that I am writing this book right now. You must block out time into your schedule for what matters to you. I am specifically writing this portion of the book at 1:40 pm while sitting next to our pool and listening to the beautiful sound of our flowing waterfall.

What does the Bible say about work?

The word "work" means "worship" in Hebrew and the word "worship" means "work" in Hebrew.

> "And the Lord God took the man, and put him into the garden of Eden to dress it and to keep it."

» **GENESIS 2:15**

https://www.biblegateway.com/passage/?search=Proverbs%2016%3A27-29&version=KJV

NOTABLE QUOTABLE

"Whatsoever ye do, do it heartily, as to the Lord, and not unto men; knowing that of the Lord ye shall receive the reward of the inheritance: for ye serve the Lord Christ."

» **COLOSSIANS 3:23-24**

https://www.biblegateway.com/passage/?search=Colossians%203%3A23-24&version=KJV

THE 6TH DAY PRINCIPLE

"To Create Like the Creator You Have to Work 6 Days."

» **CLAY CLARK**

NOTABLE QUOTABLE

"And God saw everything that he had made, and, behold, it was very good. And the evening and the morning were the sixth day."

» **GENESIS 1:31**

https://www.biblegateway.com/passage/?search=Colossians%203%3A23-24&version=KJV

NOTABLE QUOTABLE

"[1] Thus the heavens and the earth were finished, and all the host of them. [2] And on the seventh day God ended his work which he had made; and he rested on the seventh day from all his work which he had made. [3] And God blessed the seventh day, and sanctified it: because in it he had rested from all his work which God created and made."

» GENESIS 2: 1-3

https://www.biblegateway.com/https://www.biblegateway.com/passage/?search=Colossians%20 3%3A23-24&version=KJV

Where did the concept of the 4 day work week come from?

Klaus Schwab and the World Economic Forum are pushing the concept of the 4-day work week, surveillance under the skin, limiting the consumption of meat, 15-minute cities, and virtually every agenda item that would make the Anti-Christ proud:

https://www.weforum.org/agenda/2022/05/5-reasons-the-4-day-work-week-could-be-the-future-of-work/

In case you missed it...

FUN FACT:

Where did the concept of the 40 hour work week come from?

The socialist President Franklin Delano Roosevelt and his lesbian wife introduced the concept of the 40 hour work week in 1938 via the Fair Labor Standards Act -

https://en.wikipedia.org/wiki/Fair_Labor_Standards_Act_of_1938

Where did the concept of not working at all and the redistribution of income via Universal Basic Income come from?

Klaus Schwab and the World Economic Forum are pushing the concept of Universal Basic Income as the ultimate path to "financial inclusion."

https://www.weforum.org/agenda/2020/04/covid-19-universal-basic-income-social-inequality/

WHAT DOES THE BIBLE SAY ABOUT NOT WORKING?

"¹⁰ For even when we were with you, this we commanded you, that if any would not work, neither should he eat. ¹¹ For we hear that there are some who walk among you disorderly, working not at all, but are busybodies. ¹² Now those who are such we command and exhort by our Lord Jesus Christ, that with quietness they work, and eat their own bread."
II Thessalonians 3:10-12

"²⁷ An ungodly man diggeth up evil: and in his lips there is a burning fire. ²⁸ A froward man soweth strife: and a whisperer separateth chief friends. ²⁹ A violent man enticeth his neighbor, and leadeth him into the way that is not good." **Proverbs 16:27-29**

> "The soul of the sluggard desireth, and hath nothing: but the soul of the diligent shall be made fat." **Proverbs 13:4**

> "But if any provide not for his own, and specially for those of his own house, he hath denied the faith, and is worse than an infidel." **1 Timothy 5:8**

> "The hand of the diligent shall bear rule: but the slothful shall be under tribute." **Proverbs 12:24**

Now, my friend, it is time for you to buy or build a massive whiteboard, that way you can document the workflow at your business in a way you and others can understand and improve upon. How do you build a massive whiteboard affordably?

WATCH THIS VIDEO ON YOUTUBE by Michael Mila
How To Make A 4'x8' Dry Erase Board For $20 -
WATCH https://www.youtube.com/watch?v=8r6Lm1y_diY

- **BLOCK OUT SPECIFIC TIME** on the calendar for working on your business. Why? Listen to this show if you still need to know why.
https://www.thrivetimeshow.com/business-podcasts/design-sustainable-schedule/

- **DIAGRAM YOUR WORKFLOW** on your whiteboard working from left to right so you can see your biggest limiting factor at all times.
See the example below:
https://www.dropbox.com/s/6rig7moi08k8xue/Workflow%20Diagram%20of%20Sales%20-%20Version%208%20-%20EITR.psd?dl=0

1. **Marketing**
2. **Sales**
3. **Service Delivery**
4. **Human Resources Accounting**

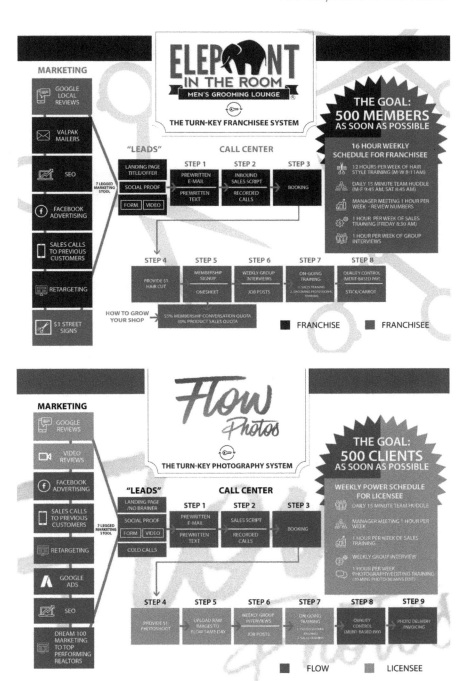

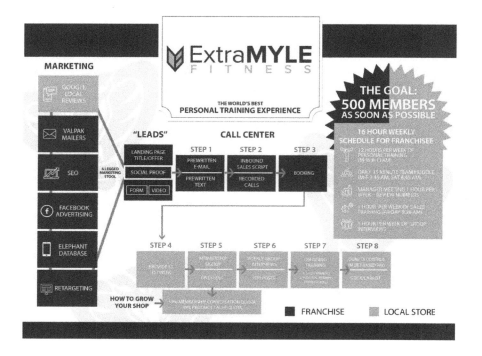

 LISTEN TO THE PASTOR of One of America's largest churches teaching how to create repeatable systems: HOW TO CREATE REPEATABLE PROCESSES AND HOW TO DESIGN A LINEAR WORKFLOW -

WATCH - https://www.thrivetimeshow.com/business-podcasts/create-repeatable-processes-design-linear-workflow/

 LISTEN TO THE AUDIO TRAINING on how to create systems - PASTOR CRAIG GROESCHEL | GROWING FROM A 2-CAR GARAGE TO 100,000 PEOPLE AND 350 MILLION DOWNLOADS.

LISTEN https://www.thrivetimeshow.com/business-podcasts/pastor-craig-groeschel-growing-from-a-2-car-garage-to-100000-people-and-350-million-downloads/

NOTABLE QUOTABLE

"I typically recommend in the early stages of organizational growth you need to go higher on control and lower on flexibility because you haven't developed a system yet where people know how to think for themselves, so you're going to think for them and be heavy on systems."

» **PASTOR CRAIG GROESCHEL**

(The founder and pastor of Life Church, which is the largest Protestant Church in America. Today Life Church has over 100,000 members who attend the 30 + campuses, and over 350 million people who have now downloaded their YouVersion Bible App.)

Back to the meat. Something tells me it's been at least a few minutes since we last discussed the concept of losing weight and feeling great as a result of deciding to only eat meat. However, at the risk of being repetitive, I want to communicate the 4 steps to successfully implementing the EXTREME and the proven path to successful weight loss on the Carnivore Diet.

STEP 1 -
Only eat meat.

STEP 2 -
Only drink coffee or water.

STEP 3 -
Don't eat anything other than meat.

STEP 4 -
Don't drink anything other than coffee or water.

As I obsessively eat only meat while writing about only eating meat, I find that eating only meat is challenging to do because it includes only eating meat. I'm not sure if the implementation of repetition is difficult. I'm not sure if boredom is an issue. But I have found in business and in all areas of life the greats bore down, while the rest of the world struggles with boredom.

"PUT ALL OF YOUR EGGS IN ONE BASKET, AND WATCH THAT BASKET."
- ANDREW CARNEGIE

(The man who built the Carnegie Steel Company,
sold it to J.P. Morgan for $480 million, and spent the
later part of his life dedicated to philanthropy.)

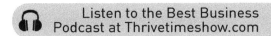
DAY 13

DETERMINE YOUR UNIQUE VALUE PROPOSITION AND YOUR PURPLE COW

When we began Elephant In The Room Men's Grooming Lounge I was 100% confident that we were not the first people on the planet to start a high-end men's grooming lounge experience. In fact, Tulsa was filled with examples of failed men's grooming lounge experiences. So, I wanted to make sure the men's grooming lounge experience that we offered our customers was 100% unique and wowing to our ideal and likely buyers. How did I do that? How can you do that?

First, you must determine your **NO-BRAINER** offer. What is the offer you are going to make to your potential first time customers that is so good that it blows their minds?! As an ample example that the average human mind can handle, at Elephant In the Room, your first haircut is just one dollar!!! Why? Because it wows our ideal and likely buyers!

Why is the company named Elephant In The Room? It's named Elephant In The Room because the Elephant In The Room is that most men dislike their haircut and the haircut experience they are currently enduring every time they decide to cut their hair, chop their mop, trim the lettuce, and remove hair from their craniums.

NOTABLE QUOTABLE

"Boring is invisible. Remarkable people and products get talked about."

» **SETH GODIN**

(Seth Godin is an iconic entrepreneur, best-selling author of 18 books including *Purple Cow*, and the man who in 1998 sold his company Yoyodyne to Yahoo! for $30 million dollars.)

THE PURPLE COW CHECKLIST

1. What is your Unique Service Offering?
(See Elephant in the Room Experience, MakeYourDogEpic.com)

2. What is your Unique Product Offering?
(See DrZoellner.com, Z66AA.com, MakeYourDogEpic.com)

3. Describe your Unique Decor:
(See Rainforest Cafe, Krispy Kreme)

4. Describe your Unique Music / Ambiance:
(See Victoria Secret, Howl at the Moon, H&M)

5. Describe your Unique Experience: (See Wholefoods, Samples Everywhere)

6. Describe your Unique Smell:
(See Starbucks, Auntie Ann's Pretzels, Godiva)

7. Describe your Unique Branding
(See Chick-Fil-A, Purple Cow, Harley, Starbucks)

8. Give Back:
(Tom's Shoes: Buy a pair, give a pair!)

9. Deep Empathy:
(SouthWest.com, Quiktrip.com)

10. Experience:
(Early Southwest Airlines Uniforms, Dick's Last Resort & Bar, Howling at the Moon)

FUN FACT: CLAY CLARK'S THRIVETIMESHOW PODCAST HAS HIT #1 ON THE ITUNES PODCAST CHART SIX TIMES

You must stand out in this cluttered world of commerce or you will lose.

AMPLE EXAMPLES:

Hobby Lobby - This company is an arts and crafts company that is unapologetically Christian. Hobby Lobby leans politically to the right. When you walk into a Hobby Lobby you will find people that are conservative and Christian in their values.

Toms.com - This is a shoe company that gives away a pair of shoes every time they sell a pair of shoes.

Harley Davidson - This is a SUPER LOUD AND BIG American made motorcycle brand.

Wholefoods - Wholefoods is a grocery store that does not apologize for their prices and hard-left-leaning politics. When you go inside Wholefoods you will run into politically left leaning people.

Starbucks - Starbucks offers high-quality beverages and food that is typically served by the most far left progressive employees they can find. If you are looking for a bearded lady, go to a circus or Starbucks.

» What is your unique selling proposition?

» What are the sights and visuals that will be featured in your business?

» What are the smells that will be featured in your business?

» What musical ambiance will you feature in your business?

» Where will your business be located?

"THIS PRODUCT IS SO GOOD IT WILL SELL ITSELF."
– SOMEONE STUPID

You must create a solid no-brainer that offers a high amount of value so that an IDEAL AND LIKELY BUYER with sound in mind could absolutely not resist the power of the offer you are making. We will beat any competitor's price by 10%. For example, our first haircut for just $1.00, first dog training lesson for 50 cents, etc.

Are you not sure how you can get out in the clutter of commerce?

 Listen to this podcast and get unstuck. FINDING YOUR NICHE | CREATING A BUSINESS THAT STANDS OUT IN A CROWDED MARKETPLACE.

https://www.thrivetimeshow.com/business-podcasts/finding-your-niche-creating-a-business-that-stands-out-in-a-crowded-marketplace/

Are you unsure of what no-brainer offer to provide your ideal and likely buyers?

 Listen to the audio training on how to create a no-brainer offer that will wow you ideal and likely buyers - DETERMINE A NO-BRAINER THAT WILL APPEAL TO YOUR IDEAL AND LIKELY BUYERS

Listen https://www.thrivetimeshow.com/business-podcasts/determine-no-brainer-will-appeal-ideal-likely-buyers/

It's time for another meet up about meat. As in the game of business, simplicity scales, and complexity fails. If you want to optimize your health and you want to implement the proven Carnivore Diet created by Thrivetime Show guest and best-selling author Doctor Shawn Baker, you need to implement the 4 steps of this EXTREME and proven path to weight loss known as the Carnivore Diet.

STEP 1 -
Only eat meat.

STEP 2 -
Only drink coffee or water.

STEP 3 -
Don't eat anything
other than meat.

STEP 4 -
Don't drink anything other
than coffee or water.

Why do the business coaching clients that I work with experience massive success?

My clients grow because I teach them the proven processes for successful strategized systems. These have been shown to work and I help them actually apply and implement what they are learning for less money than it costs to hire a minimum-wage employee.

FUN FACT: CLAY CLARK'S THRIVETIMESHOW PODCAST HAS HIT #1 ON THE ITUNES PODCAST CHART SIX TIMES

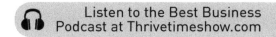

DAY 14

CREATE WORLD-CLASS BRANDING AND IMPROVE YOUR EXISTING BRANDING

. . . .

People do judge a book by its cover. People do judge people based upon their appearance. People do determine how much they are willing to pay for something based upon the packaging and that is a fact. So take a moment to ask yourself on a scale of 1 to 10 (with 10 being the highest), how highly would you rank your business on the following branding items:

YOUR WEBSITE
(on a scale of 1 to 10 with 10 being the highest)

1 2 3 4 5 6 7 8 9 10

YOUR BUSINESS CARDS
(on a scale of 1 to 10 with 10 being the highest)

1 2 3 4 5 6 7 8 9 10

YOUR IN-STORE SIGNAGE
(on a scale of 1 to 10 with 10 being the highest)

1   2   3   4   5   6   7   8   9   10

YOUR EXTERIOR SIGNAGE
(on a scale of 1 to 10 with 10 being the highest)

1   2   3   4   5   6   7   8   9   10

YOUR AUTO WRAPS
(on a scale of 1 to 10 with 10 being the highest)

1   2   3   4   5   6   7   8   9   10

YOUR SOCIAL MEDIA PRESENCE
(on a scale of 1 to 10 with 10 being the highest)

1   2   3   4   5   6   7   8   9   10

YOUR ONLINE REPUTATION
(on a scale of 1 to 10 with 10 being the highest)

1   2   3   4   5   6   7   8   9   10

YOUR MARKETING VIDEOS
(on a scale of 1 to 10 with 10 being the highest)

1   2   3   4   5   6   7   8   9   10

YOUR EXPLAINER VIDEOS
(on a scale of 1 to 10 with 10 being the highest)

1 2 3 4 5 6 7 8 9 10

YOUR ONLINE ADVERTISEMENTS
(on a scale of 1 to 10 with 10 being the highest)

1 2 3 4 5 6 7 8 9 10

YOUR ONE SHEETS
(on a scale of 1 to 10 with 10 being the highest)

1 2 3 4 5 6 7 8 9 10

YOUR MARKETING BROCHURES
(on a scale of 1 to 10 with 10 being the highest)

1 2 3 4 5 6 7 8 9 10

YOUR IN-STORE FIRST IMPRESSION
(on a scale of 1 to 10 with 10 being the highest)

1 2 3 4 5 6 7 8 9 10

YOUR IN-OFFICE FIRST IMPRESSION
(on a scale of 1 to 10 with 10 being the highest)

1 2 3 4 5 6 7 8 9 10

YOUR OVER-THE-PHONE FIRST IMPRESSION
(on a scale of 1 to 10 with 10 being the highest)

1 2 3 4 5 6 7 8 9 10

YOUR SOCIAL MEDIA MARKETING
(on a scale of 1 to 10 with 10 being the highest)

1 2 3 4 5 6 7 8 9 10

YOUR UNIFORMS
(on a scale of 1 to 10 with 10 being the highest)

1 2 3 4 5 6 7 8 9 10

YOUR OFFICE AMBIANCE
(on a scale of 1 to 10 with 10 being the highest)

1 2 3 4 5 6 7 8 9 10

YOUR PACKAGING
(on a scale of 1 to 10 with 10 being the highest)

1 2 3 4 5 6 7 8 9 10

Once you have objectively analyzed the quality or lack thereof of your branding you must do something about it.

The reason why I charge my business coaching clients $1,700 (as of the time I am writing this) and usually a small percentage of the overall business growth is because I am 100% confident that I know what I am doing. To me growing a business has always been easy and growing a business can be easy for you as long as you stay focused on bringing Big Overwhelming Optimistic Momentum to the execution of a proven path and a business plan.

QUICK FINANCIAL PRO-TIP:

As a quick pro tip, don't cheat on your business partners financially, and don't cheat on your wife sexually. Having worked with thousands of real clients to help them grow their real businesses, I am always shocked that the VAST MAJORITY of problems that occur within a business have everything to do with humans choosing to make poor life choices such as cheating on their business partners financially and cheating on their spouses sexually.

Remember, money is just an amplifier. Suppose you are a perpetually disorganized and scheming person, who is always trying to sexually score with women because of money. In that case, It will just amplify who are you with more money.

DETER MEND
MEDIOCRITY PL.
NOWHERE, UTAH

CLAY CLARK
777 SUCCESS AVE.
74119 TULSA, OK

"Be like a postage stamp. Stick to it until you get there."
–Harvey Mackay
(Businessman, best-selling author, and syndicated columnist with Universal Uclick.)

NOTABLE QUOTABLE

"If you give someone a present, and you give it to them in a Tiffany box, it's likely that they'll believe the gift has higher perceived value than if you gave it to them in no box or a box of less prestige. That's not because the receiver of the gift is a fool. But instead, because we live in a culture in which we gift wrap everything — our politicians, our corporate heads, our movie and TV stars, and even our toilet paper. Public Relations is like gift wrapping. Let's say I came to visit you today, and I brought your wife a gift. If it was in a Tiffany box, in her mind, the gift would have a higher perceived value if I gave it to her without a box or in a box of less prestige. Now, the reason that impact is true is not because your wife is a jackass. It is true because she lives in a culture where people gift-wrap everything. So we gift wrap our politicians, our corporate heads, our movie and TV stars, and even our toilet paper."

» MICHAEL LEVINE

(Michael is an American author and public relations expert. Despite growing up in an alcoholic home and being dyslexic he became the most celebrated public relations expert of all-time. Throughout Michael's career he has worked with 58 Academy Award winners, 34 Grammy Award winners, and 43 *New York Times* best-sellers including: Prince, Michael Jackson, Barbra Streisand, President Ronald Reagan, President George H. W. Bush, President Clinton, Nancy Kerrigan, George Carlin and countless other super successful people.)

"All super successful people, have a burning, maniacal rage as if their life depended on it, which I refer to as obsession."

» MICHAEL LEVINE

(Michael is an American author and public relations expert. Despite growing up in an alcoholic home and being dyslexic he became the most celebrated public relations expert of all-time. Throughout Michael's career he has worked with 58 Academy Award winners, 34 Grammy Award winners, and 43 *New York Times* best-sellers including: Prince, Michael Jackson, Barbra Streisand, President Ronald Reagan, President George H. W. Bush, President Clinton, Nancy Kerrigan, George Carlin and countless other super successful people.)

Anything that customers see must be excellent and you want to limit the number of marketing materials that you must verify are excellent. Focus on perfecting your marketing materials until everything is perfect. It would be better to have one super effective and strategic "One Sheet" versus having 12 brochures that constantly need to be updated and that are never used.

FUN FACT:

"81% of Shoppers Conduct Online Research Before Buying."

https://www.adweek.com/performance-marketing/81-shoppers-conduct-online-research-making-purchase-infographic/

Now, you must gather 10 video testimonials from real people on the real planet earth who have good things to say about you, your product, and your service as soon as possible. Why? Because your ideal and likely buyers will do their research before deciding to work with you or not. Want to learn more? Listen to the following training about the power of gathering objective online reviews until your head explodes with confidence that gathering objective Google reviews and video reviews is a great idea!

Listen - ONLINE REVIEWS 101 | WHY GATHERING REVIEWS MATTERS

https://www.thrivetimeshow.com/business-podcasts/online-reviews-101-gathering-reviews-matters/

NOTABLE QUOTABLE

"Simplicity scales, complexity fails."

» **STEVE JOBS**

(Co-founder of Apple, the former CEO of PIXAR, etc.)

Take a moment right now and go to www.ThrivetimeShow. com and click on the testimonials button. There you will find a treasure trove of literally thousands of real client testimonials and success stories. Go to www.EITRLounge.com and check out the thousands of real client case studies and testimonials that we have available there as well. Visit www.MakeYourDogEpic.com and see the countless video reviews we archive on the website. Why do we do this? We do this because it works.

FUN FACTS & Client Success Story:

How Did Clay Clark Help Ryan Wimpey to Grow TipTopK9.com?

"The search engine definitely helped. I wasn't implementing a DREAM 100. It doesn't matter how good you are if you aren't getting enough leads. Checklists for our bootcamps, processes, and structure and outlines for our private lessons, for our take home training, the sales script, and the call center scripts. Sitting down and line item by line item creating those scripts for the call center and sales was probably the biggest thing. It used to take me six months to do what we do in 6-8 weeks now. What we did with Clay, every week we come in and say this is what broke, this is what broke." - Ryan Wimpey (The Founder of TipTopK9.com)

WHAT DID CLAY CLARK & RYAN WIMPEY FIRST WORK ON TO GROW TIPTOPK9.COM?

"We did a logo first, got business cards, fliers, and then once you got the look we started making the website match the look. Autowrap and then all of our sales sheets, all of our fliers we got rid of the word documents. It doesn't matter how good you are at your craft if you don't have repeatable systems and they are not scripted out you are not going to succeed in replacing yourself. We tripled our income while growing to 17 locations. That was in 5 years. I could not have done that without hard systems." - Ryan Wimpey

HOW DID CLAY CLARK HELP TO GROW TIPTOPK9.COM?

"He's been working with so many different industries on systemizing every single part of them, that sometimes it takes a few times to hear something just like The Bible. It's really actionable information." - Ryan Wimpey

"They are just truly remarkable people. We love Clay, everything they have done for us. We would highly recommend them to anyone." - Ryan Wimpey

"We just want to give a huge thank you to Clay & Vanessa Clark. We worked with several different business coaches in the past and they were all about helping Ryan sell better, and just teaching sales, which is awesome, but Ryan is a really great salesman, so we didn't need that. We needed somebody to help us get everything that was in his head out into systems, into manuals and scripts and actually build a team. So now that we have systems in place we have gone from one location to ten locations in only a year." - Rachel Wimpey (Co-Owner of www.TipTopK9.com)

"They are so effective. If you don't use Clay and his team you are probably going to be pulling your hair out or you are going to be spending half of your time trying to figure out the online marketing game."

- Rachel and Ryan Wimpy
(Co Owners of www.TipTopK9.com)

"We appreciate you and how far you have taken us. We have gone from 1 location to 10 locations in only a year. In October of 2016 we grossed $13K for the whole month, right now, it's 2018, the month of Oct, it's the 22nd, we've grossed $50K. We are just thankful for you, and your mentorship. We are really thankful that you guys have helped us to grow a business that we run now instead of the business running us. So thank you, thank you, thank you times one thousand!"

- Ryan Wimpey
(Co-Owner of www.TipTopK9.com)

"if you don't use Clay Clark & his team you are probably going to be pulling your hair out or spending half of your time trying to figure out the online marketing game. You would be missing out on time & financial freedom."

- Ryan Wimpey
(Founder of www.TipTopK9.com)

WHAT DID CLAY CLARK DO FOR RYAN WIMPEY'S TIPTOPK9.COM BUSINESS?

"When I Was Learning to Become a Dog Trainer We Didn't Learn Anything About Internet Marketing or

SEE THOUSANDS OF CLAY CLARK CLIENT SUCCESS STORIES TODAY AT THRIVETIMESHOW.COM/TESTIMONIALS

Advertising at all. That's what is so great about working with clay. They do it all for us! They are so enthusiastic!"

- Ryan Wimpey
(Founder of TipTopK9.com)

"When I was learning to become a dog trainer we didn't learn anything about internet marketing or advertising at all. Clay has helped us to make us new logos, scripts for phones, scripts for emails, text messages."

- Ryan Wimpey

HOW DID CLAY CLARK CHANGE RACHEL WIMPEY'S MINDSET?

"My name is Rachel Wimpey. I've learned so much. I feel like my head is about to explode. Working on your business, instead of in your business because I have a tendency to just want to do it all myself. That's one thing that Clay really teaches is to have systems in place that you don't have to be there and your business can actually run without you. It's like an entrepreneur's playground. It's amazing here. It's really awesome. Clay's presentation and his style are just so different from most. It's been really one on one. He takes the time to answer your questions about your business, rather than just a generic answer. You implement those very same systems that he has discovered throughout all of the business he's run and it's just a lot of good information, really good presentation. If you don't come (to Clay Clark's business growth workshop) you are just going to be missing out on so much. Knowledge that is applicable.

It's very hands-on. There is no upsell. Most business conferences are very, very expensive, this one is very affordable, it is definitely worth it. It will completely change your mindset. It will change your life. It's definitely worth it."
- Rachel Wimpey of www.TipTopK9.com

HOW DID CLAY CLARK CHANGE RYAN WIMPEY'S MINDSET?

"I am Ryan Wimpey, I am originally from Tulsa, born and raised here. I definitely learned a lot about life design and making sure that the business serves you. The linear workflow for us and getting everything out and documented on paper is really important. We have workflows that are kind of all over the place so having a linear workflow and seeing that mapped out on multiple different boards is pretty awesome. That's pretty helpful for me.

The atmosphere here is awesome. I definitely just stared at the walls figuring how to make my facility look like this place. This place rocks. It's invigorating, the walls are super...it's very cool. The atmosphere is cool. The people are nice. Very good learning atmosphere. I literally want to model it and steal everything that is here (at Clay Clark's office) at this facility and just create it just on our business side.

Clay is hilarious. I literally laughed so hard that I started crying yesterday. The content is awesome off the charts! It's very interactive and you can raise your hand. The wizard teaches, but the wizard interacts and he takes questions and that is awesome. If you are not attending the conference you are missing three quarters to half of your life! You are missing the thought process. Just getting in the thought process of Clay Clark to me, just that is priceless. That's money!

There are no upsells or anything. The cost of this conference is quite a bit cheaper than business college. I went to a small private liberal arts college and got a degree in business and I didn't learn anything like they are teaching here. I didn't learn linear workflows, I learned stuff that I'm not using and I haven't been using for the last 9 years. So what they are teaching here is actually way better than what I got at business school and I went to what was actually ranked as a very good business school. The information that you are going to get is just VERY VERY beneficial and the mindset that you are going to get."

- Ryan Wimpey (Founder of TipTopK9.com)

HOW DID CLAY CLARK HELP RYAN WIMPEY TO SCALE HIS BUSINESS?

"Clay really helped us with his systems, taking us to the point of having ten or more employees, or doubling our size, helped us double our incomes." - Ryan Wimpey

Read the Original Full Story of How Clay Clark Mentored & Helped Ryan Wimpey to Grow & Scale TipTopK9.com HERE: https://www.justtulsa.com/business-coach-tulsa-thrivetime/4/

LEARN HOW TO START AND GROW A BUSINESS BY LISTENING TO THE THRIVETIMESHOW.COM PODCAST TODAY!

139

In this next session, I got to sit in while Clay met with a client who specializes in custom vehicle wrapping (like a vinyl wrap that gets put on over the paint on your car, ya know?)

This was another name that I was familiar with, so it was pretty cool to meet the man in charge.

This meeting was heavily themed around tracking results for some different keywords that the Thrivetime business coaching program was helping this client to rank for.

Like the others, this meeting ended up with some performance tweaks to be made to the client's website that will nearly guarantee the client's business to show up higher for the keywords that he wants to show up for in Google.

RYAN WIMPEY OF WWW.TIPTOPK9.COM SHARES WHAT HE LEARNED AT CLAY CLARK'S THRIVETIME SHOW CONFERENCE

The Tip Top K9 Dog Training Interview & TipTopK9.com Growth Story

At the conclusion of the aforementioned meeting, we step out of The Box That Rocks and Clay begins and starts his next meeting. Between the meetings, we get a brief chance to discuss the prior meeting's action points and the "how's" and "why's" of how those apply to growing a business into the best version of itself.

At this point, a couple in yellow shirts come in. They're from a company that has gone through a tremendous amount of growth since starting to work with Clay and the crew: Tip Top K9.

Clay offered to let me bounce a few questions off of them after the meeting. Once they finished up, Tip Top K9 founder Ryan Wimpey came over to where I was waiting so I recorded a few questions that I asked him.

I'm going to transcribe this conversation to text, so I'll keep it fairly abbreviated for the sake of our collective sanities.

Tyler (Just Tulsa): So, the first time I had ever heard of Tip Top K9 was back around September in one of the Thrivetime business conferences. How long have you all been working with the Thrivetime business coaching program?

Ryan Wimpey of TipTopK9.com Dog Training: We've been working with them for 14 months or so now... Just a little bit over a year.

Tyler: And how did you all get hooked up with them?

Ryan Wimpey of TipTopK9.com Dog Training: I heard about the Thrivetime business coaching program when I heard Clay on a podcast called the Profit First Podcast. I was like, "Aw, this is good!", then I was like "Wait, this guy is from Tulsa?"

Watch Clay Clark's Interviews With Profit First Podcast Founder, Mike Mikalowitz:

Tyler: How has your business changed since you first started working with Clay?

Ryan Wimpey of TipTopK9.com Dog Training: It's definitely gotten a lot better. We've got a lot of systems and marketing in place now. I don't even worry about marketing anymore.

Tyler: So, does Thrivetime business coaching program handle that or do they just kind of get you all set up and let you all handle it from there?

Ryan Wimpey of TipTopK9.com Dog Training: Nope — they handle all of our marketing.

Tyler: Really?

Ryan Wimpey of TipTopK9.com Dog Training: Yeah. They do our YouTube ads, Facebook ads, re-targeting, and Google AdWords.

Tyler: And you feel like those marketing channels bring in a worthwhile amount of leads or business?

Ryan Wimpey of TipTopK9.com Dog Training: Oh yes — last week was actually our biggest week in terms of leads, ever.

Tyler: Of those marketing channels that you guys use to get in front of your ideal customers, what does your "Three-Legged Marketing Stool" consist of? (Note: this "three-legged marketing stool refers to an approach that Clay and Dr. Zoellner teach to make sure the high quality leads come in and sustainably keep doing so.)

Ryan Wimpey of TipTopK9.com Dog Training: Ours consists of our "Dream 100", search engine optimization, and AdWords.

[At this point, me and Ryan chat for a few minutes about how inexpensive pay-per-click advertising is between Google and social media these days.]

Ryan Wimpey of TipTopK9.com Dog Training: YouTube is working wonders for us right now. They made a great video for us.

Tyler: And when that gets in front of a prospect who has been to your website before (Note: aka re-targeting/re-marketing), you're only showing your ad to people that are likely to be interested in dog training in Tulsa to begin with, right?

Ryan Wimpey of TipTopK9.com: Exactly.

Tyler: During the last conference that I went to, Clay mentioned that you all were in the beginning phases of franchising out the Tip Top K9 model to some people in Idaho. Can you elaborate on that a little bit, please?

Ryan Wimpey of TipTopK9.com: We actually have a location in Owasso that just opened this week and we've got a location in Twin Falls, Idaho. We've got another location opening in Boise, Idaho in about 3 months.

TipTopK9 Dog Training Franchisee Brett Denton Shares How Implementing Clay Clark's Turn-Key Business Systems Has Helped Him to Grow & Scale Multiple Successful Businesses.
https://rumble.com/v2ft2hk-dog-training-learn-how-to-achieve-time-freedom-and.html?mref=pk4ld&mrefc=13

Tyler: Wow. That's gotta be insane to see a business that you started — the uniforms, the van, everything — being used by someone in a completely different state.

Ryan Wimpey of TipTopK9.com Dog Training: It is! Right now, we have 9 other trainers and 2 admin people, so looking back, it's crazy to think about how at one point I was doing the whole thing by myself out of a van.

Tyler: That's crazy...

Ryan Wimpey of TipTopK9.com Dog Training: I know — Clay really helped us with his systems, because — while we could get to 4 or 5 people — taking us to the point of having ten or more employees, or doubling our size, helped us double our incomes.

[At this point, me and Ryan start talking about our mutual adoration for the book The E-Myth Revisited. I won't bore you with the details of that little tangent.]

Tyler: How was working with the Thrivetime business coaching program key in bringing you all to the point of where you are now launching multiple franchise operations?

Ryan Wimpey of TipTopK9.com Dog Training: If I never had been able to step out of the day-to-day grind, I would've never had time to build the systems that have let us replace ourselves (referring to him and his wife, Rachel). So, she was able to work on the management systems and call center stuff, and I was able to train the trainers and come up with systems for private lessons and everything else. We were really able to pull back on our involvement because we were able to systemize everything. We don't have to worry about our marketing or our website. And when we have a coach who we have to stay accountable to on a weekly basis... It helps tremendously.

Tyler: Well, I'll let you all get back to working on your business! Thanks for your time!

Ryan Wimpey of TipTopK9.com Dog Training: Thanks!

If you need additional action-step filled training on how to improve the branding of your business check out the following podcast: **OPTIMIZING YOUR BRANDING MATERIALS** - https://www.thrivetimeshow.com/business-podcasts/optimizing-branding-materials/

Many people on the planet earth create a website that does not convert website visitors into actual viable leads. Don't let this happen to you. Listen to the podcast on how to create a website that generates leads **HOW TO CREATE A LEAD GENERATING WEBSITE** - https://www.thrivetimeshow.com/business-podcasts/create-lead-generating-website/

Implementing the Carnivore Diet has been mind-freeing for me, and it is repetitive, which is what success looks and feels like. You must always remember that simplicity scales and complexity fails in all areas of life. We must find a proven plan and relentlessly implement it until we achieve success and beyond.

Knowing that there are simply 4 steps to successfully implementing the EXTREME and proven path to successful weight loss on the Carnivore Diet has been certainly mind-freeing.

STEP 1 -
Only eat meat.

STEP 2 -
Only drink coffee or water.

STEP 3 -
Don't eat anything other than meat.

STEP 4 -
Don't drink anything other than coffee or water.

NOTABLE QUOTABLE

"Success seems to be connected with action. Successful people keep moving. They make mistakes, but they don't quit."

» **CONRAD HILTON**

(The legendary founder of the Hilton Hotel and Resort chain.)

"IN A CROWDED MARKETPLACE, FITTING IN IS FAILING. IN A
BUSY MARKETPLACE, NOT STANDING OUT IS THE SAME AS
BEING INVISIBLE."
– SETH GODIN

(Seth Godin is an iconic entrepreneur, best-selling
author of 18 books including Purple Cow, and the
man who in 1998 sold his company Yoyodyne to
Yahoo! for $30 million dollars.)

Quick Note:

*I know that it has been a minute, but I wanted
to bring it up again for good measure. Soon and
very soon we must actually sell something for
a profit to your ideal and likely buyers. If you
can't sell your business, it will begin to money
bleed and you will not succeed.*

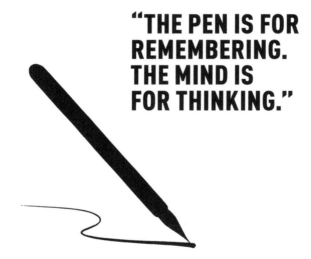

"THE PEN IS FOR REMEMBERING. THE MIND IS FOR THINKING."

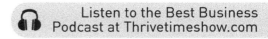

DAY 15

LAUNCH YOUR 4-LEGGED MARKETING STOOL

What is a 4-legged marketing stool? You want to figure out the 3 or 4 best ways to reach your ideal and likely buyers and then you want to aggressively implement this strategy as fast as possible while accurately tracking the results.

» **Define** what you think is going to work.

» **Act** upon what you believe will work.

» **Measure** the results of the marketing campaign you launched.

» **Refine** the marketing efforts you are implementing.

» **Perfect until perfect.**

Now it is time to market your product to your ideal and likely buyers. Thus, you must determine, who are your ideal and likely buyers?

- Who are the humans on this planet that will actually want to buy products and services from you?

- Are you primarily marketing to men or women?

- Where do your ideal and likely buyers live?

- Where do your ideal and likely buyers go during the day?

You must not waste your hard-earned money marketing to the wrong audience.

When we started Elephant In the Room Men's Grooming Lounge, it became very clear that most of my employees at my other businesses did not appreciate or like having a high-end men's grooming lounge experience and that was fine. However, we needed to market the high-end men's grooming services that we offered to our ideal and likely buyers and our ideal and likely buyers were as follows:

We marketed to men.

We marketed to men who were between 25 and 60 years old via social media.

We launched mailers to target homes worth more than $400,000.

We launched our social media ads to only reach people that lived within 10 minutes of the men's grooming lounge.

We made sure that our first location at the 16th and Boston in Tulsa was physically located near the workplace of men who had well-paying jobs.

DESCRIBE YOUR IDEAL AND LIKELY BUYER

Write your answers on this page. Remember, if your ideas are not documented and stuck in your head then your business dreams will always stay dead.

1. **Men or Women or Both?**
   _____

2. **Average Age?**
   _____

3. **Average Income Level?**
   _____

4. **Geographical Location?**
   _____

5. **Places They Go?**
   _____

6. **Schools Their Kids Attend?**
   _____

7. **Search Terms They Type Into Search Engines?**
   _____

8. **Shared Fears?**
   _____

LEARN HOW TO START AND GROW A BUSINESS BY LISTENING TO THE THRIVETIMESHOW.COM PODCAST TODAY!

151

9. Shared Goals?

_____

10. Shared Hobbies and Interests?

_____

11. Shared Problems?

_____

12. Sports Their Kids Play?

_____

13. Stores They Shop At?

_____

14. Types of Cars They Drive?

_____

15. Proven Ad, Landing Page, Set Budget

_____

NOTABLE QUOTABLE

"Lazy hands make for poverty, but diligent hands bring wealth."

» PROVERBS 10:4

(The Bible)

WHAT WAS THE 4-LEGGED MARKETING STOOL WE USED TO LAUNCH THE ELEPHANT IN THE ROOM MEN'S GROOMING LOUNGE?

Leg #1
Search Engine Domination

Leg #2
Signs & Wonders That Draw the Attention of Our Ideals And Likely Buyers As They Drive By.

Leg #3
Social Media Advertisements Launched On Facebook & Instagram Targeted At Our Ideal & Likely Buyers

Leg #4
Mailers to Our Addresses of Our Ideal And Likely Buyers

4-Legged Marketing Stool

AMPLE EXAMPLES

DR. ZOELLNER'S OPTOMETRY

- Radio Ads
- Mailers
- Google Reviews
- Physical Location/Signs & Wonders

ELEPHANT IN THE ROOM

- Search engine optimization
- Signs & Wonders
- Social Media Advertisement
- Valpak Mailers

Remember your marketing will not work if you do not offer your customers a solid no-brainer offer that is so hot, so exciting and so compelling that your ideal and likely buyers can simply not resist it. When we offered the $1 first haircut at Elephant In The Room, we began generating interest and leads from our ideal and likely buyers. You must have a powerful no-brainer offer.

Advertising for your business is like adding gasoline to your car. Advertising to your business is like oxygen, food and water to humans. You must advertise your business. If you want to learn more about the importance of on-going effective and powerful advertising listen to this interview with the legendary public relations consultant of choice for Michael Jackson, Prince, Nike, Pizza Hut and more today HERE:

WHY YOU MUST ADVERTISE TO CREATE GROW A BUSINESS CAPABLE OF PRODUCING BOTH TIME AND FINANCIAL FREEDOM – ASK CLAY ANYTHING

https://www.thrivetimeshow.com/business-podcasts/why-you-must-advertise-to-create-grow-a-business-capable-of-producing-both-time-and-financial-freedom-ask-clay-anything/

If you want to learn more about the importance of launching retargeting advertisements that follow your website visitors all around the internet after they have visited your website, listen to the podcast on why you can never stop advertising from the co-founder of the 700 + employee business, Adam Berke with Adroll

- GAME-CHANGING ADVICE...WHERE MOST PEOPLE GET IT WRONG WITH THEIR STRATEGIC MARKETING | THE ADAM BERKE AND ADROLL STORY – PT. 2

https://www.thrivetimeshow.com/business-podcasts/game-changing-advice-where-most-people-get-it-wrong-with-their-strategic-marketing-the-adam-berke-and-adroll-story/

How much should you spend on advertising? You should spend the least amount possible while still aggressively marketing your business. Listen to Michael Levine, the Public Relations and marketing consulting of choice for President Bush, President Clinton, Nancy Kerrigan, Nike, Pizza Hut, Charlton Heston, Prince, and Michael Jackson explaining that the fastest growing companies in the world on average spend 11% of their budget on marketing.

ART OF GRINDING EVERY WEEK & SPENDING 11% OF YOUR BUDGET ON MARKETING (WITH PR GURU MICHAEL LEVINE)

https://www.thrivetimeshow.com/business-podcasts/art-grinding-every-week-spending-11-budget-marketing-pr-guru-michael-levine-2/

Want to learn more about the process of launching an effective and stable three-legged marketing stool? Listen the the podcast on how to launch a sustainable three-legged marketing stool - **HOW TO LAUNCH SUSTAINABLE 3 LEGGED MARKETING STOOL**

https://www.thrivetimeshow.com/business-podcasts/launch-sustainable-3-legged-marketing-stool/

How do you launch **Google Adwords, Adroll retargeting advertisements, Facebook advertisements, Instagram ads, Youtube Ads** and more? Listen to the Thrivetime Show Podcast until your head explodes.

FUN FACTS

"90% of consumers read online reviews before visiting a business."

https://www.forbes.com/sites/ryanerskine/2017/09/19/20-online-reputation-statistics-that-every-business-owner-needs-to-know/#416ee1ddcc5c

"91% of online adults use search engines to find information on the web."

https://www.forbes.com/sites/ryanerskine/2017/09/19/20-online-reputation-statistics-that-every-business-owner-needs-to-know/#416ee1ddcc5c

If you are going to market a business on the planet Earth today you must have a fully optimized website that generates leads.

If you cannot generate leads your business cannot succeed which is why we are now going to obsessively focus on teaching you how to optimize your website.

"EVERYTHING ELSE BECOMES UNNECESSARY IN A BUSINESS IF NOBODY SELLS ANYTHING."
– CLAY CLARK

(Founder of ThriveTimeShow.com, former U.S. SBA Entrepreneur of the Year, host of the ThriveTime Show, and America's #1 Business Coach.)

In order for you to achieve total SEARCH ENGINE DOMINATION and DRAMATICALLY increase your level of COMPENSATION you must simply check off and complete all of the checklist items on this website evaluation. We humbly refer to this checklist as "The Ultimate Search Engine Domination Checklist."

The Ultimate Search Engine DOMINATION Checklist
(and Website Evaluation):

_____ **Host your website with a reliable hosting service**. If your website is hosted with an unreliable hosting service you will rank lower in the search engines. We recommend using GoDaddy.com. Don't host your website with some local, janky hosting provider who lives with his mom in the basement.

_____ **Host your website with the fastest package that you can afford.** Google REALLY CARES about how long it takes for your website to load. Why? Because people get impatient and will quickly move on to another website if your website takes too long to load. On January 17th of 2018, Google formally announced the "Speed Update." Google's plan called for them to slowly roll out the new search engine ranking criteria to give web-developers plenty of time to make their websites load much, much faster. To test the speed of your website visit: https://developers.google.com/speed/pagespeed/insights/ To read more about Google's new speed requirements visit: https://www.forbes.com/sites/jaysondemers/2018/01/29/will-googles-new-page-speed-criteria-affect-your-site/#396634ed6a8f

____ Build your website on the WordPress platform.
"WordPress offers the best out-of-the-box search engine optimization imaginable." - Tim Ferriss (Best-selling author of *The 4-Hour Work Week*, *The 4-Hour Body*, *The 4-Hour Chef*, *Tools of Titans,* and *Tribe of Mentors*. He is also an early stage investor in Facebook, Twitter, Evernote, Uber, etc.)

Don't use any other website building platform than WordPress. If you hire coders to custom build your website on PHP or .NET you will end up hating your life as a result of having a website that nobody can update other than the entitled, nefarious employees who now have the ability to hold you hostage. Trust us here. We have personally coached hundreds of clients and every time our coaching clients have a custom built website the business owner at some point has been held hostage by the employee who is the only person who knows how to update the custom built, non-search engine friendly, and ridiculously complicated website. Building your website on WordPress puts the power back in your hands as a business owner because you can update the website yourself if you have to.

PRO TIP: USE WORDPRESS.ORG NOT WORDPRESS.COM

WordPress.org is the open source platform used to power the best SEO compliant websites in the world. WordPress.com is their platform that does not allow for plugins or optimal website optimization.

*Avoid WordPress.com

_____ Build a mobile-friendly website. What is a mobile friendly website? Check your website's mobile compliance at: https://search.google.com/test/mobile-friendly. If this link changes in the future just search for "Google mobile compliance test" in the Google search engine and you'll find it.

_____ Install HTTPS encryption onto your website.
HTTPS encryption stands for Hypertext Transfer Protocol Secure. What does that mean? HTTPS encryption makes your website more difficult for bad people to hack, thus making it tougher for very bad people to crash your website and to use your website as a way to steal the personal information of your valuable clients and patrons. Google ranks websites higher who have invested the additional money needed to add HTTPS encryption to their website. How many times would you use Google if every time their search results sent you to websites that had been hacked into by cyber criminals and internet hackers?

 _____Install the Yoast.com search engine optimization plugin into your website. What is Yoast? Yoast SEO is the best WordPress plugin on the planet when it comes to search engine optimization. Yoast was built and designed in a way to make search engine optimization approachable for everyone, and thus we love Yoast. Yoast makes it possible for people who are not complete nerds to proactively manage the search engine optimization of their website.

 DEFINITION MAGICIAN
Plugin - A plugin is a piece of code or software that provides a variety of functions that you can add to your WordPress website. Plugins allow you to increase the functional capacity of your website without having to hire a bunch of nefarious, entitled custom coders who are typically hard to manage because you do not have any idea what they are working on or what they are talking about 90% of the time.

_____Uniquely optimize every meta title tag on every page of your website.

The title tag is simply a hypertext markup language (HTML) element on a website that specifies to search engines what a particular web page is all about. "according to SEOMoz, the best practice for the title tag length is to keep titles under 70 characters." An example would be, "Full Package Media | Dallas Real Estate Photography | 972-885-8823"

Full Package Media | Dallas Real Estate Photography | 972-885-8823
https://fullpackagemedia.com/ ▾
Looking for the best in the business when it comes to Dallas Real Estate Photography? You need to

_____Uniquely optimize every meta description on every page of your website. The meta description is simply part of the hypertext markup language (HTML) code that provides a brief summary about a web page. Search engines like Google usually show the meta description in search engine results. Don't make your meta descriptions more than 160 characters in length.

An ample example would be, "Looking for the best in the business when it comes to Dallas Real Estate Photography? You need to call Full Package Media today at 972-885-8823."

Looking for the best in the business when it comes to Dallas Real Estate Photography? You need to call Full Package Media today at 972-885-8823.
Careers · About Us · Contact Us · Client Login

_____Uniquely optimize the keywords on every page of your website. Meta keywords are a very specific kind of meta tag that will show up in the hypertext markup language (HTML) code on web pages and these will tell the search engines what the web page is really all about. An example of specific keyword optimization would be "Berj Najarian." You may be thinking, who is Berj Najarian?

LEARN HOW TO START AND GROW A BUSINESS BY LISTENING TO THE THRIVETIMESHOW.COM PODCAST TODAY!

Berj Najarian serves as the New England Patriots Director of Football and the "Chief of Staff" for the legendary Coach Bill Belichick who has won a total of 8 Super Bowl titles since beginning his coaching career in the National Football League. If someone is searching for "Berj Najarian" there is a high probability that they already know who "Berj Najarian" is and if you want to rank high in the search engines when people are searching for "Berj Najarian" you definitely want to make sure that you have declared your meta keyword phrase as "Berj Najarian."

Quick Note: If at any point while reading this you are beginning to feel overwhelmed just submit your website for an audit and deep dive evaluation and we'll do the heavy lifting for you. You can submit your website to be audited at: www.ThrivetimeShow.com/Website

 _____ **Create 1,000 words of original and relevant text (content) per page on your website.** Are we saying that somebody actually has to write, 1,000 original words of original and relevant text for every page of your website? Yes. Isn't there a hack? NO. Can't there be a better way? No.

Can't you just go out and hire a company out of India to use "spinners" to slightly change existing text for you? NO. Can't you just copy content from another website? NO.

You can spend every minute of every day trying to find some blogger or some website experts out there that will tell you that someone on your team doesn't need to invest the time needed to create 1,000 words of both original and relevant content and you will eventually find them and they will be 100% wrong. However, they will gladly take your money.

YOU OR A MEMBER OF YOUR TEAM MUST WRITE
1,000 WORDS OF ORIGINAL AND RELEVANT
CONTENT FOR EVERY PAGE OF YOUR WEBSITE.

_____ **Create a Google search engine compliant
.XML sitemap on your website.** What is an .XML
sitemap? XML stands for Extensible Markup Language.
A quality XML sitemap serves as a map of your website
which allows the Google search engine to find all of
the important pages located within your website. As a
website owner unless you hate money, you REALLY WANT
GOOGLE to be able to crawl (find, rank, and sort) all
of the important pages on your website. Yoast.com has
tools that will actually generate Google compliant .XML
sitemaps for you. Don't worry, you can do this!

Fun Fact: *I had to take Algebra 3 times en route
to getting into Oral Roberts University and I
was eventually kicked out of college for writing
a parody about the school's president "ORU
Slim Shady" which you can currently find on
YouTube. If I can learn and master search engine
optimization you can too!*

  SEE THOUSANDS OF CLAY CLARK CLIENT SUCCESS
STORIES TODAY AT THRIVETIMESHOW.COM/TESTIMONIALS

_____Create a Google search engine compliant HTML sitemap. What's an HTML site map? A hypertext markup language sitemap allows the people who visit your website to easily navigate your website. This sitemap should be located at the bottom of your website and should be labeled as a "Sitemap."

Hiding your sitemap for any reason is a bad idea because Google assumes that if you are hiding your sitemap you are probably trying to hide something. Don't change the background of your website to be the same color as your sitemap's font or do anything tricky here. You want to make sure that your website's sitemap can easily be found at the bottom of your website. See the example below:

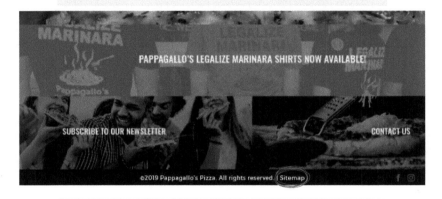

_____Create a clickable phone number. If you ever want to sell something to humans on the planet Earth you must make your contact information easy to find. Thus you want to make your phone number easily available to find at either the top right or at the bottom of your website. When coaching your web-developer, force them to make your phone number a "click-to-call" phone number so that users on your website who are using a mobile phone (almost everyone) can simply click the number to call you.

In our shameless attempt to make this the BEST, MOST HUMBLE and the MOST ACTIONABLE SEARCH ENGINE OPTIMIZATION book of all time we have provided the following real examples from REAL clients just like you who we have really helped to REALLY increase their REAL sales year after year:

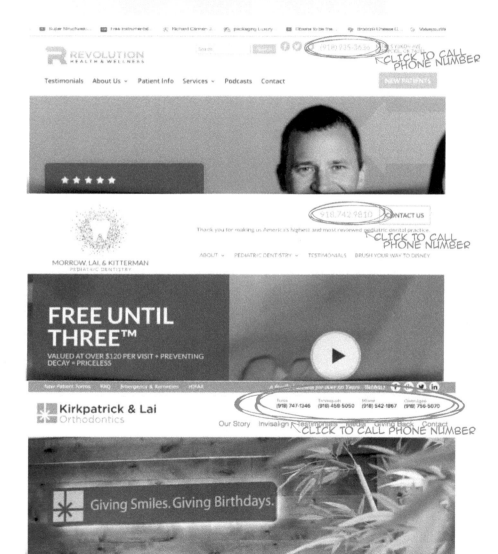

_____**Have a Social Proof.** If you don't hate money and you are not a committed socialist, you will want to include some social proof near the top of your website. What is social proof? "Social proof" is a phrase and a term that was original created by the best-selling author Robert Cialdini in his book, ***Influence***. The best social proof examples are:

a. Real testimonials from real current and former clients is super powerful.

b. Media features and appearances on credible media sources like Bloomberg, Fox Business, Entrepreneur.com, Fast Company, etc.

c. Proudly showing that you have earned the highest and most reviews in your local business niche.

d. Celebrity endorsements from celebrities that have earned the trust of your ideal and likely buyers.

e. Listed below is an example that will showcase to you what it looks like to use social proof effectively.

_____Make the logo return to home. Allow the logo on your website to serve as your "homepage" button. As of 2019, most people assume that if they click your logo they are going to be taken back to the homepage of your website.

_____Create original content. You must create more original and relevant content than anyone else in the world about your specific search engine focus. If you want to come up top in the world for the phrase "organic supplements" you must then create the most original and relevant content on the planet about "organic supplements." If you want to come up top in your city for the phrase "knee pain Tulsa" then you must what? You must create the most original and relevant content on the planet about "knee pain Tulsa."

If you want to come up top in the search engine results for the phrase "America's #1 business coach" then you must create the most original and relevant content on the planet about "America's #1 business coach." Listed below are a few examples of receiving high search rankings due to having the most original, relevant content on the planet about that particular subject.

---

america's #1 business coach

All   News   Images   Videos   Maps   More   Settings   Tools

About 5,870,000 results (0.35 seconds)

Business Coach | Bill Belichick's #1 Fan and America's #1 Business ...
https://www.thrivetimeshow.com/the...show/business-coach-management-principles/ ▾
★★★★★ Rating: 99% - 2,651 votes
Bill Belichick's number one fan and America's #1 business coach Clay Clark teaches many of the
successful management principles that Belichick ...

People also ask

Who is the best business coach in the world?   ⌄

What should I look for in a business coach?   ⌄

1.3 mi · 3019 E 101st St · (918) 299-4415 ext. 5384

WEBSITE   DIRECTIONS

The Little Gym of SE Tulsa
4.7 ★★★★✬ (14) · Gymnastics center
3.3 mi · 6556 E 91st St · (918) 492-2626
Open · Closes 7.30PM
🌐 Their website mentions **gymnastics classes**

WEBSITE   DIRECTIONS

Twist & Shout Tumbling & Cheer
3.5 ★★★✬✩ (8) · Gym
6.2 mi · 4820 S 83rd E Ave · (918) 622-5867
Closed · Opens 5PM
🌐 Their website mentions **tumbling classes**

WEBSITE   DIRECTIONS

≡ More places

Tumbling Tulsa | Tulsa Tumbling Lessons | 918-764-8804
https://justicetumblingco.com/ ▾
If you are looking for the best and highest reviewed **tumbling Tulsa** place, you need to call us at Justice
Tumbling today and see what makes us better.
Services · About · Schedule · Testimonials

Tulsa Cheerleading | Tumbling Tulsa | Tulsa Tumbling | 918-986-5785
https://tumblesmart.com/ ▾
Tulsa's Most Reviewed **Tumbling** Program. **Tumble** Smart Athletics. Free Evaluation **Lesson**Meet the
Owner. **Tumbling Tulsa** Gymnast Stars. Experience the

Google   tulsa knee pain   🎤   🔍

META TITLE TAG

Tulsa Knee Pain - Revolution Health Tulsa
https://www.revolutionhealth.org/.../tulsa-knee-pain-revolution-health-is-bring-in-a-re... ▾
PERMALINK   Find the best treatment for your **Tulsa knee pain** right here in Tulsa. Find out more about Revolution
Health by calling at 918-935-3636.   META DESCRIPTION

Tulsa knee Pain | Revolution Health Oklahoma
https://www.revolutionhealth.org/.../tulsa-knee-pain-find-the-top-and-quickest-result-f... ▾
The best prolotherapy is right here at Revolution Health for **Tulsa knee pain**.

Best Prolotherapy Treatments Tulsa | Tulsa Knee Pain
https://www.revolutionhealth.org/.../tulsa-knee-pain-find-the-best-possible-tulsa-knee-... ▾
Best Cure Best Prolotherapy Treatments for your **tulsa knee Pain**.

Non-invasive remedies relieve knee pain without surgery - Tulsa World
https://www.tulsaworld.com/...knee-pain.../article_6bdf681d-d017-554c-9ecc-fae529... ▾
Mar 13, 2019 - Dear Doctor K: I have osteoarthritis of the knee. Are there ways to relieve my **knee pain**
without drugs or surgery?

_____Create a "Testimonials," "Case Studies," or a "Success Stories" portion of your website if you want to sell something to humans who were not born yesterday. Most shoppers today have become savvy and are aware of the fact that great companies generate great reviews (and occasionally bad ones) and that bad companies chronically generate bad reviews (and occasionally some good ones). Thus, most people will want to actually see testimonials, case studies or success stories from real clients that have actually worked with your company in the past.

In fact, not having testimonials, case studies, and success stories on your website freaks most people out to the point that they won't even call you or fill out your contact form.

How do we know this? Well, for starters, we are humans who happen to be also consumers and Forbes tells us that, "Almost 90% of consumers said they read reviews for local businesses. In other words, if you are not investing efforts into online reputation management, then you are missing out on having control of the first impression your business has." - *Online Reviews and Their Impact On the Bottom* Line by Matt Bowman - https://www.forbes.com/sites/forbesagencycouncil/2019/01/15/online-reviews-and-their-impact-on-the-bottom-line/#35d3b4955bde

NOTABLE QUOTABLE

 "Perfectionism is often an excuse for procrastination."

- PAUL GRAHAM
(The entrepreneur investor, incubator, and coach behind AirBNB, Dropbox, and Reddit)

_____**Include a compelling 60-second video / commercial (on the top portion above the fold) on your website** to improve your conversion rate. To provide you with an ample example of clients that we have personally worked with who have used a "website header video" in route to dramatically increasing their sales check out:

_____**Create a "top of the website" call to action** that

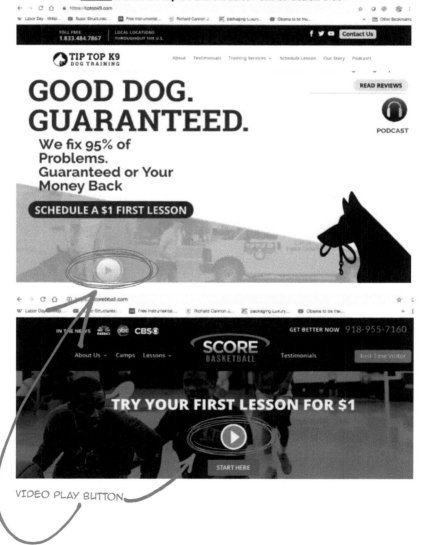

VIDEO PLAY BUTTON

your ideal and likely buyers will relate to and connect with. You want to make it SUPER EASY for your ideal and likely buyers to call you, to schedule an appointment with you, or for them to do business with you in the most convenient way possible. As an AMPLE EXAMPLE check out EITRLounge.com and OXIFresh.com:

CALL TO ACTION

CALL TO ACTION

_____ **Create a "No-Brainer" sales offer deal** that is so GOOD, so HOT, and so IRRESISTIBLE that your ideal and likely buyers simply cannot resist the urge to at least try out your services and products out. As an example, we would encourage you to check out the following websites.

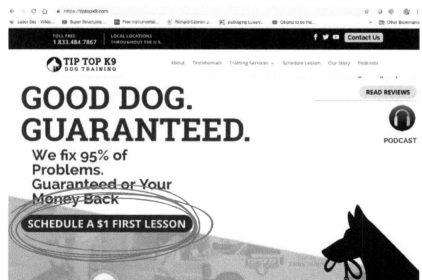

Learn everything you need to know about search engine optimization by listening to my EPIC two-part interview with a man known as the "The Father of Search Engines" and the best-selling author of Search Engine for Dummies, Bruce Clay.

THE MILLION DOLLAR PODCAST | SEARCH ENGINE OPTIMIZATION WITH THE FATHER OF SEARCH ENGINE OPTIMIZATION, BRUCE CLAY (PART 1 OF 2)

https://www.thrivetimeshow.com/business-podcasts/the-million-dollar-podcast-search-engine-optimization-with-the-father-of-search-engine-optimization-bruce-clay-part-1-of-2/

(Part 2 of 2) THE MILLION DOLLAR PODCAST | SEARCH ENGINE OPTIMIZATION WITH THE FATHER OF SEARCH ENGINE OPTIMIZATION, BRUCE CLAY

https://www.thrivetimeshow.com/business-podcasts/pt-2-the-million-dollar-podcast-search-engine-optimization-with-the-father-of-search-engine-optimization-bruce-clay/

Now that you have learned how to create a search engine compliant website, you now must make it happen.

Do you want your ideal and likely buyers to actually find you in the search engine results?

You must commit yourself to achieving the following 4 action steps related to your website as soon as possible.

1 You must create a Google canonically compliant website.

2 You must create a Google mobile compliant website.

3 You must gather two times more objective Google reviews than you closest competitor.

4 You must write two times more original HTML (hypertext markup language) keyword optimized content than your competition.

Note: The reason why I include web development, search engine optimization, online advertisement, management, sales coaching, videography, photography, speaking, coaching, and more for our clients is that ideas are easy. Implementations are hard and all I care about is implementation.

••

How do you create more content than your competition?

Listen to the podcast about the importance of creating more original HTML content than your competition.
HOW TO WRITE THE CONTENT FOR YOUR WEBSITE

https://www.thrivetimeshow.com/business-podcasts/write-content-website/

How do you gather two times more objective Google reviews from real people on the planet Earth? Listen to the podcast about the importance of gathering objective Google reviews - **ONLINE REVIEWS 101 | WHY GATHERING REVIEWS MATTERS**

https://www.thrivetimeshow.com/business-podcasts/online-reviews-101-gathering-reviews-matters/

NOTABLE QUOTABLE

"It takes 20 years to build a reputation and five minutes to ruin it. If you think about that, you'll do things differently."

» **WARREN BUFFETT**

(The founder of Berkshire Hathaway who is regarded by many as the most successful investor in American history.)

Now back to that conversation that we were having about the Carnivore Diet. The biggest challenge about following it is that you and I must only eat meat. The diet has been proven to work, but nothing works unless we do. The big question is then, if we know what to do why don't we just do it? If we know that eating a high-protein and low-carb diet is the key to optimizing our health, why don't we just follow the simple proven plan? The Carnivore Diet is repetitive, which is what success looks and feels like. You must always remember that simplicity scales and complexity fails in all areas of life. We must find a proven plan and relentlessly implement it until we achieve success and beyond.

Knowing that there are simply 4 steps to successfully implementing the EXTREME and proven path to successful weight loss on the Carnivore Diet is both mind-freeing and incredible!!!

STEP 1 -
Only eat meat.

STEP 2 -
Only drink coffee or water.

STEP 3 -
Don't eat anything
other than meat.

STEP 4 -
Don't drink anything other than coffee or water.

We are now getting to the point where you must sell something to your ideal and likely buyers in exchange for a sustainable profit margin. Your goal is to WOW your customers with a wonderful product or service in exchange for a profit that is a true win-win between you and your customers.

As an example, at MakeYourDogEpic.com we are experiencing EPIC amounts of growth because the services we provide our customers are affordable and mind-blowing. The first dog training lesson is just 50 cents, we will beat any competitor's price, we offer the fastest turn-around time, we are the highest rated and most reviewed dog trainers in America, we offer a money-back guarantee and you earn a chance to win a trip to Hawaii just by hiring us at MakeYourDogEpic.com!

NOTABLE QUOTABLE

"Render more service than that for which you are being paid and you will soon be paid for more than you render."

» **NAPOLEON HILL**

(Best-selling author of *Think and Grow Rich*.)

LEARN HOW TO START AND GROW A BUSINESS BY LISTENING TO THE THRIVETIMESHOW.COM PODCAST TODAY!

175

FUN FACT:

Did you know that OXIFresh.com the brand that
I haved worked with for 17+ years now has more
objective Google reviews than nearly any other
service business on the planet? Do a google search
for "Carpet Cleaning Quotes" and you will see that
OXIFresh.com now has over 270,000 objective
Google reviews from our real customers.

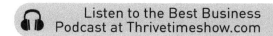
DAY 16

CREATE A SALES CONVERSION SYSTEM THAT GENERATES RESULTS

. . . .

It has taken me 26 years to find and organize the knowledge contained in this book and also the Thrivetime Show Podcast. When I grew up poor, I always wished that there was a resource, a mentor or a guide that I could go to that would teach me the proven paths to super success. That is what this is. Additionally, I have made all 30+ of my books available for FREE to read and download today at: www.ThrivetimeShow.com/millionaire.

As you listen to my podcast just know that you are learning practical and proven advice from some of the most successful people on the planet including:

» The former Executive Vice President of Walt Disney World Resorts who was once responsible for managing over 40,000 employees and 1,000,000 customers per week at the world's most successful tourist venue.

» The pastor of the largest Protestant church in America today, Craig Groeschel (founder of Life Church)

 » The public relations consultant of choice for some of the world's most iconic businesses and celebrities, Michael Levine, including Michael Jackson, Prince, Nike, Charlton Heston, Cameron Diaz, President Clinton, Nancy Kerrigan, etc.)

 » The two-time Olympic gold medal winner, two-time NBA Champion, one-time MVP turned successful entrepreneur and investor, David Robinson.

 » The former Chief Communications Officer for Harley Davidson, Ken Schmidt, who famously helped to lead the company's turnaround from 1985 to 1999.

 » One of the world's most respected psychologists, who is the *New York Times* best-selling author of the legendary book, *Emotional Intelligence.*

 » One of the world's most respected financial advisors and the 9 x *New York Times* best-selling author. Throughout his career, David Bach, has been featured on *Oprah*, the *Today Show, Fox News*, and countless media outlets throughout his career.

If you ever get stuck simply email us at info@ThrivetimeShow.com and I shall assist you down the proven path either as a one-on-one business coaching client, as a conference attendee or as a podcast listener. Now back to sales conversion 101! In order to convert your leads into actual paying customers you must create the following documents:

FUN FACT: CLAY CLARK'S THRIVETIMESHOW PODCAST HAS HIT #1 ON THE ITUNES PODCAST CHART SIX TIMES

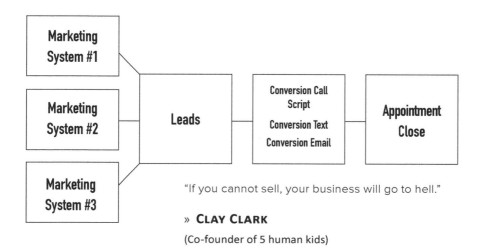

"If you cannot sell, your business will go to hell."

» **CLAY CLARK**

(Co-founder of 5 human kids)

 You must create **standardized call scripts** so your employees know what to say to your ideal and likely buyers.

 You must install **call recording**. I recommend a company and service called www.ClarityVoice.com

 You must nail down and determine **standardized pricing** for your business.

 You must install a **lead tracking system** so that you know where all of your leads and buyers are coming from. You must ask all of the leads how they ORIGINALLY heard about you!!!

 You must track your **sales conversion system**. What percentage of leads do you close?

You must install all of these **tracking systems** because what you treasure you must measure. Everything that you measure expands other than your waistline!

FUN FACTS

"The U.S. Chamber of Commerce estimates that 75% of employees steal from the workplace and that most do so repeatedly."

READ - https://www.cbsnews.com/news/employee-theft-are-you-blind-to-it/

"85% of Job Applicants Lie On Resumes."

READ - https://www.inc.com/jt-odonnell/staggering-85-of-job-applicants-lying-on-resumes-.html

You must create a **unified database** of all of your current customers, past customers, and inbound leads.

You must also operate your business with a mindset that is filled with paranoia. You must not trust the people who work for you unless you want to be robbed blind. What? Yes. Only the paranoid survive.

As I teach you all of you this, you must know that you will face endless adversity and crimes against humanity as a business owner. You will be screwed and sued. You will be slandered and attacked online for holding employees accountable. However, just know that as you encounter this adversity you are not alone. All successful business owners have to deal with human drama and jackassery.

Now back to the Elephant In the Room story. Did you throughout the course of starting, growing, and running The Elephant In The Room Men's Grooming Lounge for the past 13 years that the following events have happened related to employees and more:

An employee slept with a woman that he was not married to while he was working as the employee's manager.

An employee used the company credit card to buy lingerie from Victoria's Secret.

An employee bought a large truck using the company's name without the consent of the ownership.

An employee routinely stole cash out of the cash registers.

An employee lied about their hair license, their real name, and their entire background story.

An employee left to start his own company to directly compete with us.

An employee left and attempted to hire away all of our staff.

An employee left and attempted to take away all of our customers.

An employee got drunk with a woman he was managing at a Christmas party and decided to spend the night with her while he was still married to another woman.

A key manager kept arriving late to his staff meetings while then showing up late with his mistress, while openly married to someone else.

An employee stole cash tips constantly.

In order to keep control of your business and to prevent yourself from being robbed blind all of the time you must do the following:

» Install video cameras in your business

» Install call recording via ClarityVoice.com in your business

» Look at your weekly numbers and assume that someone is stealing from you every day.

» Have a daily huddle with your team so that you can look them in the eyes and determine who is stealing from you today.

» You must track all spending on company credit cards to catch waste and fraud.

You must learn how to become a master salesperson to win in the game of business and you must learn how to create and implement a proven turn-key sales system that allows other members of your team to sell well in a scalable manner. To learn sales conversion 101 from one of the world's top sales trainers ever. Listen to my interview with the late great sales trainer and the author of *Soft Selling In a Hard World*, Jerry Vass HERE: **HOW TO SOFT SELL IN A HARD WORLD WITH MASTER SALES TRAINER JERRY VASS.**

LISTEN - *https://www.thrivetimeshow.com/business-podcasts/how-to-soft-sell-in-a-hard-world-with-master-sales-trainer-jerry-vass/*

We Can Either Learn from Mentors, Mistakes, or Mistaken-Mentorship

Having been self-employed since the age of 16, I can tell you from first-hand knowledge that learning by trial and error is too painful and expensive. It just takes too long. We all know we can either learn from mentors and mistakes, yet most of us don't know where to go to get answers we're seeking. Any entrepreneur with a semi-functional mind sincerely believes that your "network is your net worth." However, what should we do if we are surrounded by negative people who have the wealth-repelling habits, attitudes and mentalities and we don't have access to millionaire mentors and billionaire buddies? Where do you start to get effective mentorship in this world of charlatans and wealth-building scammers?

NOTABLE QUOTABLE

"If you are not doing hard things, you are doing the right things."

» **LEE COCKERELL**

(ThriveTimeShow.com Mentor and former Executive Vice President of Walt Disney World Resorts who once managed over 40,000 employees. Many years ago, I also helped Lee provide his legendary book called *Time Management Magic*.)

False Mentorship and Get-Rich-Quick Programs Are Readily Available

At the age of 18, I was struggling to grow what would later become one of the largest wedding entertainment companies on the planet (www.DJConnection. com), I quickly discovered two powerful lessons about finding high-quality mentors.

THE B-TEAM IS READILY AVAILABLE - The slick-talking-charlatan-quack-get rich-quick-motivational-manipulators,and-no-money-down-real-estate-scammer-pyramid scheme- a-penzi-pushers are readily available at all times. In fact, they made themselves so believable to my naive brain that they were to scam me out of thousands of dollars by selling me bogus legal advice, bogus corporate strategies, bogus search engine optimization systems, bogus leadership certifications, bogus conference up-sells, and bogus book writing tips. I'm so thankful that I was only scammed out of thousands and not hundreds of thousands.

THE A-TEAM IS ALMOST NEVER AVAILABLE - Get used to it. The actual millionaires, billionaires, and everyday success stories with "real businesses" that you and I have read about, or whose businesses we actually buy things from are almost never available. The kings and queens of capitalism, who actually have the words of wisdom and the proven success strategies that we seek to learn live behind walls both figurative and literal in order to protect their time and their minds. Over time as a means of survival nearly all super successful people have become fastidious managers of time. Super successful people are very intentional about setting up both digital and physical boundaries to prevent everyone from having access to them so that they can scale their businesses while also enjoying the success that they've created in the areas of their: Faith, family, finances, fitness, friendship, and fun. Their success is not based on luck. Successful people have intentionally designed and created their success with daily self-discipline, time management, and daily diligence.

NOTABLE QUOTABLE

Walk with the wise and become wise, for a companion of fools suffers harm."

» **PROVERBS 13:20**

It will require persistence to become successful in the world of sales. You must learn how to overcome adversity and how to deal with rejection. I committed mentally to receiving countless rejections, cold-calling, emailing, and just showing up at the businesses of super-successful people until I could arrange a meeting with them to ask them the specific questions that I had. I decided to get serious about my life and to try to set up appointments with the A-TEAM OF SUPER SUCCESSFUL PEOPLE that weren't out there selling get-rich-quick programs. I decided to reach out to the G.O.A.T.(s) (The greatest of all time) and to separate myself from the B-Team charlatan false-mentors with moats (I dedicate this rhyme to the B-Team).

And the good news is that it only took me 22 years of relentless cold-calling to round up these mentors who have radically both changed and improved my life:

» Before I met and received mentorship from Doctor Robert Zoellner (The founder of Doctor Robert Zoellner and Associates, the founder of Z66 Auto Auction, the founder of A to Z Medical, one of the original investors and board members of Regent Bank, Dr. Zzz's Sleep Center) about marketing, my yellow page and digital advertisements never produced inbound sales leads.

» Before I was able to spend time with Chet Cadieux (The President of the multi-billion dollar convenience chain QuikTrip), I had no idea how to create a linear workflow, how to create repeatable processes, the critical importance of scheduling daily workouts, the value of merit-based pay, the necessity of checklists, the value of mystery shopping and that every business owner should read:

The One Minute Manager by Ken Blanchard PhD and Spencer Johnson, MD, *The Service Profit Chain* by W. Earl Sasser and Leonard A. Schlesinger, *The Value Profit Chain* by James L. Heskett (Author), W. Earl Sasser (Author), Leonard A. Schlesinger (Author), *Straight from the Gut* by Jack: Straight from the Gut.

» Before I was able to spend days with David Robinson (Two-time Gold Medal Winner, a two-time NBA Champion, and a one-time MVP of the entire NBA who has arguably been more successful off of the basketball court than on it), I did not understand the importance INTENSELY PROTECTING YOUR FAMILY BY SCHEDULING TIME IN THE CALENDAR FOR THEM AND NOBODY ELSE.

Before receiving mentorship from David Robinson, I had never fully understood the importance of truly celebrating my wife as being the gift that she truly is.

» Before meeting Maurice Kanbar (the iconic inventor

who is best known as the founder of Skyy Vodka, the owner of 50 patents, the former owner of over 25% of downtown Tulsa and the man responsible for creating the Safetyglide hypodermic needle protector) I thought that all great inventors typically only specialized in one type of invention and I had no idea what that process was like for going from an idea to an actual product that customers can buy.

» Before meeting George Foreman (The Olympic gold medalist, the two-time heavyweight boxing champion of the world), I had never met someone who had prioritized their spiritual development over their financial development like George Foreman did when he decided to retire from boxing in 1977 to become a Pastor and to give back to his local community.

» Before meeting Michael Levine (The public relations consultant of choice for Michael Jackson, Prince, President Clinton, Charlton Heston, Nike, Pizza Hut, and other A-list celebrities and Fortune 500 companies) I had no idea how much the average person really does buy and judge a book or a product based upon its' cover, its' wrapping, and its' overall branding.

NOTABLE QUOTABLE

"What good will it be for someone to gain the whole world, yet forfeit their soul? Or what can anyone give in exchange for their soul?"

» **MATTHEW 16:26**

(From that controversial and politically divisive book known as The Bible)

As You Are Leaning to Grow a Successful Business You Must Insist On Receiving Mentorship with a Moral Compass

Although this idea may not be popular in today's culture of "do-whatever-feels-good," in this book you are going to find teaching and words of wisdom from super successful people and we are not going to be teaching about:

- Moral relativity

- The power of hallucinogenic drugs

- Selling products and services that play to people's vices (alcohol, drugs, prostitution, etc.)

- Scamming people in exchange for a quick dollar

NOTABLE QUOTABLE

"We repeat the points that are important and differentiate us from the competition. Repetition is very good. In the beginning, some people rejected it in our company. They said everybody knows that that's kind of silly. I asked the question of all general managers because they're the ones who rejected it: Does everybody in the room know what Coca-Cola is? Raise your hand if you don't know. Nobody raised their hands. So you all know? So the question is, why do they still advertise? Because you have to keep it alive. You have to repeat it. That is absolutely central. If it is important, you repeat it. Make it simple, and repeat it. We do this before every shift. You cannot go into your shift without going through a 3-4 minute session. Where that point is repeated and re-explained."

» **HORST SCHULTZE**

» **HORST SCHULTZE**
(Thrivetime Show Guest and former and Chief Operating Officer of the Ritz-Carlton Hotel Company. In August 1983, Gerald W. Blakely who owned and managed the hotel sold The Ritz-Carlton Boston Hotel and the US trademark for $75.5 million to William B. Johnson who was once the largest owner of Waffle House franchises. William assembled a four-person dream team in Atlanta to lead a company headed by Horst Schulze to create the Ritz-Carlton chain of hotels established by The Ritz-Carlton Hotel Company brand in its current form. Schulze dramatically revolutionized the hotel industry while turning the Ritz-Carlton hotel company into one of the most remarkable and recognized international brands on the planet.)

A GLIMPSE INTO THE MANAGEMENT MASTERY AND WISDOM OF THRIVETIME SHOW PODCAST GUEST, HORST SCHULTZE.

"The moment someone accepts a leadership role, they have agreed to work towards accomplishing the objective of an organization. First of all, good organizations have objectives which are good for all concerned. That means the investor, the employee, the customer, and society. Now, comes an excuse right here: people will say, well, my organization is not good. That's not your decision to make when you're a leader.

You have accepted that organization's objectives, and in that moment you are responsible for finding the solutions to the situations that exist. That's the role the leader fills, and of course helps other people, the employees, to reach the objectives. I don't hire a leader to explain to me what is wrong.

I can never forget we had a budget based on 68% occupancy in the hotel in Boston, at the time. We only met 55%, so I called the leader to find out what happened. He said, "Well, the weather in Boston..." The weather. He had to create an excuse, but he would call it a reason. No, I asked him, "Wait a second. What about the Copley Plaza? What kind of business did they have?" He said, "They have been very slow."

So tell me, Did the guest arrive at the airport and say "Because it's snowing in Boston, and it's so cold I'm not going to the Ritz Carlton?" It is not so. We have no right to move immediately to an excuse. We have to find solutions. We have to say, here's what happened, here's what I'm going to do next January. You know, there is no beauty, there is no reward, there's no pleasure in the excuse. All the rewards are in the objective."

It's been at least a chapter since I have discussed it, but repeating a proven system over and over until you reach your goals is the key to achieving massive success. You and I must have self-discipline if we are going to achieve massive success. In fact self-discipline is the bridge between goals and turning those goals into reality. And thus I find myself only eating meat. Is it exciting? No. Does it work? Yes. Do I want to implement a meat-only diet? No. However, knowing that there are simply 4 steps to successfully implementing the EXTREME and proven path to successful weight loss on the Carnivore Diet is mind-freeing and incredible!!!

STEP 1 -
Only eat meat.

STEP 2 -
Only drink coffee or water.

STEP 3 -
Don't eat anything other than meat.

STEP 4 -
Don't drink anything other than coffee or water.

NOTABLE QUOTABLE

"Before anything else, preparation is the key to success."

» **ALEXANDER GRAHAM BELL**

(A Scottish-born scientist and inventor who is credited with the inventing and patenting of the world's practical telephone and founding the American Telephone and Telegraph Company (AT&T) in 1885.)

Quick Note:

We should start selling something very very soon or you will end up living in a van down by the river or learning how to make our very own "will work for food" sign using the best practice method of cardboard and Sharpies. Remember if you can't sell, your business will go to hell and your life will not go well.

"I'M A GREAT BELIEVER IN LUCK, AND I FIND THE HARDER I WORK, THE MORE I HAVE OF IT."
— THOMAS JEFFERSON
(One of the Founding Fathers and the Third President of the United States.)

FUN FACT: CLAY CLARK'S THRIVETIMESHOW PODCAST HAS HIT #1 ON THE ITUNES PODCAST CHART SIX TIMES

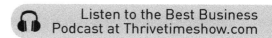
DAY 17

YOU MUST KNOW YOUR CUSTOMER ACQUISITION COST IF YOU ARE THE BOSS

When you start marketing your business you must know how much marketing money it costs you to generate a real lead who is an actual ideal and likely buyer.

When you start marketing your business you must know how much marketing money it costs to generate an actual paying customer.

Having worked with thousands and thousands of business owners directly to help start, grow, and scale a successful business, I can tell you that the vast majority of business owners simply do not know how much marketing money it costs them to generate a new customer. This is a huge problem. You must know where your customers are coming from, or you will not be able to effectively manage your finances. As a business owner, you cannot delegate your finances to somebody who is not you. You must know what is going on with the financial aspects of your business.

Remember when you are growing a business, it's not about "The Best" business. It's about the "Best-Selling Business." Nobody remembers the best-written book, however everybody remembers the "Best-Selling" books. So during this portion of the book, I'm going to insert a transcript from my interview with the best-selling co-author of the *Rich Dad Poor Dad* book series which went on to become the best-selling business book in modern history.

 Sharon Lechter is a CPA, entrepreneur, philanthropist, mother, and co-author of the *New York Times* best-selling *Rich Dad Poor Dad* book series which went on to sell 23 million copies. She served as the former CEO of the *Rich Dad* Organization and sold the first million copies of *Rich Dad Poor Dad* while the organization was still based in her home. In 2008, Sharon was asked by the Napoleon Hill Foundation to join the team to co-author multiple book projects including the best-sellers: *Think and Grow Rich-Three Feet from Gold*, *Outwitting the Devil*, *Think and Grow Rich for Women*, and *Grow Rich for Kids*.

"Well back in 1995, Robert Kiyosaki had gone to see my husband, Michael Lechter, who is an intellectual property attorney. He proposed an idea for a board game and it was drawn out on a piece of paper, but he needed somebody to help make it happen. So, he went to see my husband about getting that copyrighted and patented. In that process, I had already been working in the area of financial literacy so my husband introduced us because he thought that I would enjoy seeing the potential of the game, which I really did. I met Robert at the first beta test for times out of the game. It was drawn out on a piece of butcher block paper, and the playing was loud. These pieces were different caliber bullets. First impression is everything right? This is how I have the three tables of players, I was the only person who got out of the rat race. With time really saw the value of the messaging, which is consistent with my messaging:

Financial freedom needed to write and edit, understanding the importance of passive income, building assets, and not relying on a job or a paycheck for your financial health, so I volunteered to help him.

My background has been helping to build the audiobook industry. We also had this book an electronic game, so I had a network of influence that I could draw on with no guaranteed pay-off. As we were talking about it, Robert wanted to charge $200 for the board game. I said, well maybe we need a brochure that talks about the philosophy so that people will be convinced to invest $200. During that process, he asked me to be his partner and invest over $50,000 and 1,000 hours to write a book. The brochure ended up being *Rich Dad, Poor Dad*. We never expected it to be a huge success in its own right. It was written really as a brochure to sell the game, and of course, the world came and said, no, your brand is not only cash flow, your brand is Rich Dad. So we decided to write three books, *Rich Dad Poor Dad*, *Cashflow Quadrant*, and Guide to Investing. After we did those, people still wanted more, so we might not have written a total of 15 books during the 10 years that I was his partner. I owned the company and I led it as the CEO. Then we had a second brand of books that we'd launched - the *Rich Dad* Advisors books along with all of our other programming, so that's really how it got started. Listen to the market and provide what the market wants. However, I would highly recommend that you do not sell the world the vices that it begs for (alcohol, marijuana, cigarettes, gambling, etc...)

Robert was interested in the fact that both my background and my philosophy were consistent with his, I was a CPA, and I had the experience and the connections we needed to help build the business. So, we became partners and in 10 years we built the *Rich Dad* brand globally.

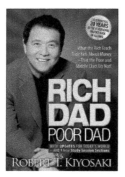

WHEN YOU WERE WRITING THE PAMPHLET FOR THE GAME, WHEN DID IT MORPH INTO THE BOOK?

Well, we said we needed a brochure, but the brochure became the book. The purpose was to tell the story, and to be able to give it to people for free. We wanted to have a $15 product that would lead to the $200 board game, and that is why it was not originally published in hardback. It was originally published in paperback.

DID YOU ACTUALLY SELL A MILLION COPIES OF A BOOK OUT OF YOUR HOUSE?

Yes, we did. We really ran the company out of my home for the first three years. In fact, our local post office got to the point where they said, Sharon, we can't handle your volume anymore. We had a local fulfillment house that would store the inventory and ship for us. But, yes, we sold the first million books and we made it to the *New York Times* best seller list out of my house. The original book was published by a company that my husband and I own called Tech Press. We did that so we could control the book; if we wanted to give it away, we could. That's not something you can do with traditional publishers. As we built that success and got on all the lists, all of the sudden, we had all these other publishers coming to us wanting to help. It was a good thing. When we really hit the stride, we received a phone call from Oprah, and we were able to do a deal with Warner Books, and the rest is history. We spent seven and a half plus years on the *New York Times* best seller list.``

YOU SOLD 26 MILLION COPIES OF THE RICH DAD BOOKS WHEN YOU WERE CEO, IS THAT CORRECT?

Of the *Rich Dad* series, yes. *Rich Dad, Poor Dad* was the greatest one, but yes. Globally, the book was translated into over 50 languages in over 100 countries.

NOTABLE QUOTABLE

"In the future, the great division will be between those who have trained themselves to handle these complexities and those who are overwhelmed by them. Those who can acquire skills and discipline their minds and those who are irrevocably distracted by all the media around them and who can never focus enough to learn."

» **ROBERT GREENE**
(Best-selling author of *Mastery, The 50th Law, The Law of Human Nature & The 48 Laws of Power*.)

In order to learn more about knowing your break-even point, listen to the following podcast: **HOW TO DETERMINE YOUR WEEKLY BREAK-EVEN AND GOAL ACHIEVEMENT NUMBERS.**

» https://www.ThrivetimeShow.com/
business-podcasts/determine-weekly-break-
even-goal-achievement-numbers/

Eating only meat has helped me to reconnect with the mindset I had while I was building DJConnection.com from the ground up out of my dorm room. Everyday I helped myself to cold-calling businesses to let them know about my startup disk jockey and entertainment service while the rest of the college campus was having a good time living the college life. I had to delay gratification and get a job working at Applebee's, Target, and DirecTV in order to raise the money needed to buy my first equipment. Was it all consuming? Yes! Was it worth it? Yes. However, eating only meat brought me back to that extreme self-discipline mindset of holding myself accountable to something I don't want to do that will not produce immediate results. We must remember that self-discipline is the bridge between goals and turning those goals into reality. And thus, I find myself only eating meat. Is it exciting? No. Does it work? Yes. Do I want to implement a meat only diet? No. However, knowing there are simply 4 steps to successfully implementing the EXTREME and proven path to successful weight loss on the Carnivore Diet is mind-freeing and incredibly effective!!!

STEP 1 -
Only eat meat.

STEP 2 -
Only drink coffee or water.

STEP 3 -
Don't eat anything
other than meat.

STEP 4 -
Don't drink anything other than coffee or water.

NOTABLE QUOTABLE

....

"You either pay now or pay later with just about every decision you make about where and how you spend your time."

» **LEE COCKERELL**

(The former Executive Vice President of Walt Disney World Resorts who once managed over 40,000 employees at the world's number tourist destination.)

Quick Note:

I hope you are selling something to your ideal and likely buyers in exchange for a profit or you will find yourself getting skinny due to the controversial, yet very effective starvation diet.

LEARN HOW TO START AND GROW A BUSINESS BY LISTENING TO THE THRIVETIMESHOW.COM PODCAST TODAY!

199

**YOUR BUSINESS EXISTS TO SOLVE PROBLEMS
FOR YOU AND YOUR CUSTOMERS.
- CLAY CLARK**

(Founder of ThriveTimeShow.com, former U.S. SBA
Entrepreneur of the Year, host of the ThriveTime Show,
and America's #1 Business Coach.)

FUN FACT: CLAY CLARK'S THRIVETIMESHOW PODCAST
HAS HIT #1 ON THE ITUNES PODCAST CHART SIX TIMES

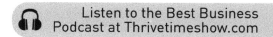

DAY 18

CREATE REPEATABLE & SCALABLE SYSTEMS THAT WOW YOUR IDEAL & LIKELY BUYERS

. . . .

It's very important that you build a system for everything. In fact, during this section of the book I am going to include many of the checklists and systems that I have created that make Elephant In The Room run successfully. **You must build repeatable systems for every aspect of the business such as:**

1. Create call scripts.

2. Create customer refund policies.

3. Create linear workflows for how the customer experience is supposed to work.

4. Create checklists for everything.

You cannot build an organization unless you are organized and you must insist that your company is organized to the point that everything has a place and every action has a documented best-practice way of doing it. I'll never forget while I was building Elephant In the Room we had a teammate who insisted on being late to everything, spelling everything wrong, using abbreviations that nobody else knew, saving files in the wrong place and refusing to follow proven systems and processes. I had to let this highly-skilled and highly-motivated person know every week that being late for the staff meeting is not acceptable and that saving files in odd places and using abbreviations that only they knew was not scalable, it was not productive and it was actually cancerous to the growth of the business. He was actually trying to scale a fail. You must be organized to grow an organization. The conversations never went well, but the business was successful because I refused to give ground to dysfunctional behavior in the business.

"MAKE A PLACE FOR EVERYTHING."
-CLAY CLARK

(Founder of ThriveTimeShow.com, former U.S. SBA
Entrepreneur of the Year, host of the ThriveTime Show,
and America's #1 Business Coach.)

NOTABLE QUOTABLE

....

"Formal education will make you a living; self-education wil make you a fortune."

» **JIM ROHN**

(*New York Times* best-selling author and iconic sales trainer.)

NOTABLE QUOTABLE

....

"Rarely do we find men who willingly engage in hard, solid thinking. There is an almost universal quest for easy answers and half-baked solutions. Nothing pains some people more than having to think."

» **MARTIN LUTHER KING, JR.**

(The man and minister who was at the center of the Civil Rights Movement in America.)

1. **You must create a universal way to save all of your files.**

2. **You must create a training system for your business.**

3. **You must create an employee interview process.**

4. **You must create a new employee on-boarding process.**

5. **You must create an employee write-up process.**

6. **You must create a checklist for everything.**

7. **You must create a proforma for your business.**

8. **You must create an income and expense documentation process for your business so that you can see where your money goes and flows.**

9. **You must create an organizational chart for your business.**

10. **You must create an inventory list for your business.**

11. **You must have a system for every aspect of your business.**

12. **You must create a system for backing up all of your files and digital documents at all times.**

13. **You must create a document that lists the contact information for all of your employees.**

14. **You must create a document that lists the contact information for all of your vendors.**

15. You must have a set time for interviewing job candidates every week.

16. You must have a set time to look at your numbers every week.

17. You must have a set time to lead your daily huddle with your employees.

18. You must have a set time to lead your weekly staff meeting.

19. You must have a set time for your weekly staff sales training.

20. YOU MUST CREATE A MASTER TRAINING SHEET. TRACK THE KEY PERFORMANCE INDICATORS THAT WILL ENSURE YOUR COMPANY IS SUCCEEDING AND NOT FINANCIALLY BLEEDING.

NOTABLE QUOTABLE

"Simplicity scales, complexity fails. People think focus means saying yes to the thing you've got to focus on. But that's not what it means at all. It means saying no to the hundred other good ideas that there are. You have to pick carefully. I'm actually as proud of the things we haven't done as the things I have done. Innovation is saying no to 1,000 things."

» **STEVE JOBS**

(The co-founder of Apple and the former CEO of PIXAR.)

If you want to learn everything you need to know about how to make effective checklists, listen to the following mind-blowing Thrivetime Show podcasts: **HOW TO SYSTEMATIZE YOUR BUSINESS BY CREATING AND IMPLEMENTING THE USE OF CHECKLISTS FOR EVERYTHING!**

LISTEN - https://www.ThrivetimeShow.com/
business-podcasts/systematize-business-creating-
implementing-use-checklists-everything/

EVERYTHING YOU NEED TO KNOW ABOUT CHECKLISTS (WITH FORMER EVP OF DISNEY, LEE COCKERELL)

LISTEN - https://www.ThrivetimeShow.com/
business-podcasts/everything-need-know-checklists-
former-evp-disney-lee-cockerell/

NOTABLE QUOTABLE

"This is not about managing your time. It is about keeping Your whole life under control. Plan the life you want or live the life you don't want..."

» **LEE COCKERELL**

(Former Executive Vice President of Walt Disney World Resorts who once managed 40,000 team members.)

FUN FACT: CLAY CLARK'S THRIVETIMESHOW PODCAST HAS HIT #1 ON THE ITUNES PODCAST CHART SIX TIMES

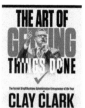

You must rename all files to remove abbreviations. If you want to learn more about how to become dramatically more organized and how to become more organized listen to this podcast: *THE ART OF GETTING THINGS DONE* (PART 3) – HOUR TWO

https://www.ThrivetimeShow.com/thrive-time-show/ art-getting-things-done-part-3-hour-two-ep-347/

You must save all of your passwords in a way that you can find them when you need them: Listen to the following podcast to find **190 MILLION REASONS TO PROACTIVELY ORGANIZE YOUR PASSWORDS AND FILES – A KNOWLEDGE BOMB** - Get all passwords stored in one universal location

https://www.ThrivetimeShow.com/ business-podcasts/190-million- reasons-to-proactively-organize- your-passwords-and-files-a- knowledge-bomb/

NOTABLE QUOTABLE

"Don't wait until everything is just right. It will never be perfect. There will always be challenges, obstacles, and less than perfect conditions. So what? Get started now. With each step you take, you will grow stronger and stronger, more and more skilled, more and more self-confident, and more and more successful."

» **MARK VICTOR HANSEN**

(The best-selling author behind the *Chicken Soup for the Soul* series of books.)

Because I always manage a roster of 160 business clients that I am coaching to victory, I have found that a very small percentage of entrepreneurs care at all about this area of growing a business. In fact, I find most entrepreneurs are perpetually distracted and disorganized in a way that causes chaos for everyone around them. If you want to get your business and life in order. However, I recommend that you listen to these powerful podcasts about how to become dramatically more organized and productive now.

CREATE DAILY CHECKLISTS FOR EVERYTHING - Listen to the podcast on the importance of creating checklists for everything -

 https://www.ThrivetimeShow.com/business-podcasts/
create-daily-checklists-for-everything/

Knowing that growing a business is easy and that weight loss is too, is actually alarming to many people.

For some reason, I have found that when people know exactly what to do, we often don't want to do it. It's really bizarre. However, what I have found is that the clients that I work with who actually want to implement the proven systems and processes that have been shown to work time and time again, become massive success stories. However, I have also discovered a unique group of people over the years that I often refer to as "ASK-HOLES." These are people that will ask for a solution, but they don't actually want a solution, they just want to discuss the problem perpetually. I want to make sure that I don't become the "ASK-HOLE" of the Carnivore Diet. It's been shown to work, however can I stay focused on the concept of only eating meat long enough to achieve my goals? That is the question. Do I crave flavor or optimal health more? Do I care more about weight loss or more about eating mindless calories that taste good? What is more important to me? However, here is a quick recap of the Carnivore Diet in case you forgot:

STEP 1 -
Only eat meat.

STEP 2 -
Only drink coffee or water.

STEP 3 -
Don't eat anything
other than meat.

STEP 4 -
Don't drink anything other
than coffee or water.

NOTABLE QUOTABLE

"There is one quality which one must possess to win, and that is definiteness of purpose, the knowledge of what one wants, and a burning desire to possess it."

» **NAPOLEON HILL**

(Best-selling author of *Think and Grow Rich* and the former speech writer to President Franklin Delano Roosevelt.)

Quick Note:

You should be at a place in your entrepreneurial journey where you recognize that if you can't sell your business will not do well.

"TEMPORARY FAILURES ARE A PREREQUISITE TO SUCCESS."
–NAPOLEON HILL

(A man who was mentored directly by the steel tycoon
Andrew Carnegie, the best-selling self-help author of all-
time during his lifetime, the author of *Think & Grow Rich,
The Law of Success, The Master-Key to Riches,* etc...)

THE TURN-KEY, PROVEN HIRING PROCESS

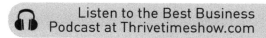

DAY 19

LEARN TO MANAGE EFFECTIVELY OR FIND YOURSELF BEING HELD HOSTAGE BY PEOPLE YOU ARE PAYING

· · · · · · · · · · · ·

Management is simply the ability to get your team to deliver great results to your customers with a spirit of excellence and over-delivery while being on-time and on budget. However, I find that management is the most difficult thing for most business owners to do. Why? Most humans want to be liked more than they like getting things done. As a business owner you must learn how to hold your team accountable.

NOTABLE QUOTABLE

"Genius is 1 percent inspiration, and 99 percent perspiration."

» **THOMAS EDISON**

(The legendary inventor whose team created the first practical light bulb, the first recorded audio, and the motion picture technology while creating General Electric.)

In order to effectively manage your team you must do the following things every week for as long as you run the business.

"THE LOWER AN INDIVIDUAL'S ABILITY TO LEAD, THE LOWER THE LID ON HIS POTENTIAL."
- JOHN MAXWELL

1- You must schedule a weekly recurring time for your weekly staff meeting.

2- You must have a daily huddle where you lay out the plan for the day.

3- You must fire the bottom 10% of your workforce and replace them with better people.

4- You must schedule a set weekly time to interview new employee candidates every week.

5- You must hold your team accountable for delivering excellent results to your customers.

6- You must not tolerate bad attitudes.

NOTABLE QUOTABLE

"You always have to remember that your Christian values are your own. You can't force that on the other people that come into your organization.

I think it's key that you build a culture so that they know what to expect. And once they come in you build a level of expectation and if they meet it, great, if they don't that's fine. Probably the best example for me is looking at my time playing with the Spurs. We brought in a guy like Dennis Rodman, as an example. Dennis, is a very unique character, you know he's not your fall in line, do everything you ask him to do kind of a guy. He really runs to the beat of his own drum, but there are certainly a lot of things he brings to the table that are outstanding and he's the best at what he does in certain areas, so you have to learn how to incorporate that into your team without detracting from what you're trying to accomplish in the big picture."

» DAVID ROBINSON

(David Robinson is a multiple time guest on the Thrivetime Show Podcast and David is a committed husband, father of three children and a former dominant National Basketball Association player. Throughout David's NBA career he was a two-time Gold Medal Winner, a two-time NBA Champion, and a one-time MVP of the entire NBA. He has continued to be one of the leading philanthropists in American sports which lead to the National Basketball Association creating the David Robinson Plaque that is now awarded to current players to recognize them for outstanding community service. Since retiring from the game of basketball, David has gone on to become arguably more successful off the court than he was on the court. He was inducted into the NBA's Hall of Fame in 2009 and he founded and funded the $9 million Carver Academy in San Antonio.)

HOW DO YOU MANAGE SOMEBODY WITHOUT BRINGING EMOTION TO IT?

"I don't think you take the emotion out, I think the emotion is important because it shows people you care about what you are doing, that you care about your organization and that you care about them. If you're emotionless, it doesn't make them feel too much like you care about what's going to happen to them, so I think you just have to temper that emotion and always understand that they are feeding off of you. You're the leader and you're the one setting the tone. So if you act wrong, you've got to expect them to start acting wrong. It's the same way with children. They're going to watch you. You are the one that is going to set that tone for that office. So when you deal with it, be full of passion for your job, passion for your company or organization and passion for the task at hand. People appreciate that and if you get upset, we could do that on the basketball court. I can get upset with somebody and get in their face, but it was never personal and that's the key. Don't make it personal, don't make it "I don't like you, I don't like what you do". Make it "this is not helpful for where we are going and if you don't get on board, you will not be going with us". In every circumstance, you're focused on the goal at hand and you're focused on trying to improve that person, you're trying to take that person a step further, but at the same time we have a big picture and if you can't catch up or if you can't run with us, then you need to always offer positive constructive and future focused criticism. NEVER make it personal, unless your goal is to no longer ever speak to them again. We all lose our cool, we all make mistakes and people understand that but you have to be strong enough to go back and say, look I'm sorry that was not right.

We can't worry about making mistakes, we are going to make those, but at the same time, if we can keep our minds focused on the goal, if we stay in tune with where we're going, and we know the direction, we will win. That's what leaders do, they lead. They set the tone. Leaders set direction and leaders carry everyone else to that place so that's why you take your most talented people and make sure they are on the same page with you."

» **DAVID ROBINSON**

(David Robinson is a multiple time guest on the Thrivetime Show Podcast and David is a committed husband, father of three children and a former dominant National Basketball Association player. Throughout David's NBA career he was a two-time Gold Medal Winner, a two-time NBA Champion, and a one-time MVP of the entire NBA. He has continued to be one of the leading philanthropists in American sports which lead to the National Basketball Association creating the David Robinson Plaque that is now awarded to current players to recognize them for outstanding community service. Since retiring from the game of basketball, David has gone on to become arguably more successful off the court than he was on the court. He was inducted into the NBA's Hall of Fame in 2009 and he founded and funded the $9 million Carver Academy in San Antonio.)

How would you rate your ability to manage your team on a scale of 1 to 10?

Create a checklist for every aspect of your business. I know that I've hammered this concept home throughout the book, but I fear that I am not doing it enough. You must create a checklist for every aspect of your business.

You must install a GPS system on all work related vehicles if you want to manage your team effectively.

As mentioned earlier, you must install call recording via **www.ClarityVoice.com** or some other vendor that you can trust.

You must install video recording in your business to verify that you are not being robbed by your employees. At Elephant In the Room, I have caught thousands and thousands of dollars of theft over the years.

You must determine you will only hire people that can bring the following 5 skills sets and mindsets to the workplace or you will spend your day managing idiots.

Energy - You must hire employees that bring great energy to the workplace.

Energize - You must hire employees that energize others and that do not create strife and division within the business.

Execute - You must hire employees that can actually get their jobs done.

Edge - You must hire employees that will do the right thing and make the tough call when you are not around.

Passion - You must hire an employee that has a passion for your life so that you don't spend your whole day managing a bunch of doom and gloom people which will suck your soul and your energy away from you.

NOTABLE QUOTABLE

"You are the average of the five people you associate with."

» TIM FERRISS

(The *New York Times* best-selling author of *The Four Hour Work Week*.)

You must not get management and leadership advice from people that don't know what they are talking about, which is most people. You must take advice from people that know what they are talking about and who know the proven path to business success. Most people can't grasp the mindset of carrying about results more than being liked. As a manager you must hold your team accountable to delivering excellence to your customers. You must seek out and fire poor performers before the customers fire you.

NOTABLE QUOTABLE

"My personal coaching philosophy, my mentality, has always been to make things as difficult as possible for players in practice, however bad we can make them, I make them."

» BILL BELICHICK

(Legendary NFL football coach of the New England Patriots.)

You must determine and post the key performance indicators for all employees to see. To learn more about the importance of managing with key performance indicators listen to this podcast: **KNOWING YOUR WHY, K.P.I.S & R.O.I.S WITH OXI FRESH FRANCHISE BRAND DEVELOPER, MATT KLINE.**

https://www.ThrivetimeShow.com/business-podcasts/knowing-your-why-k-p-i-s-r-o-i-s-with-oxi-fresh-franchise-brand-developer-matt-kline/

LEARN HOW TO MANAGE LARGE TEAMS BY LISTENING TO THESE MANAGEMENT TEACHING PODCASTS:

👍 SEE THOUSANDS OF CLAY CLARK CLIENT SUCCESS STORIES TODAY AT THRIVETIMESHOW.COM/TESTIMONIALS

Management Execution | Management Is the Ability to Get Your Team to Deliver Results to Your Customers With a Spirit of Excellence & Over-Delivery While Being On Time & On Budget + Celebrating the MoralesBrothers.net & TipTopK9.com Success Stories.

» WATCH - https://rumble.com/v4faygx-management-execution-management-is-the-ability-to.html

Learn how to properly hire, inspire, train, and retain quality people by listening to this life-changing post and interview with Lee Cockerell, the former Executive Vice President of Walt Disney World Resorts who used to manage 40,000 employees and 1,000,000 customers per week - **HOW TO INSPIRE AND RETAIN QUALITY EMPLOYEES.**

» https://www.ThrivetimeShow.com/business-podcasts/inspire-retain-quality-employees/

The waist is a terrible thing to mind. However, there is a proven weight-loss system that has been proven to work which was actually written in a book form called, The Carnivore Diet in case you forgot. This book is written by Thrivetime Show Guest, Doctor and best-selling author Doctor Shawn Baker. Here is a quick recap in case the diet plan is sounding kind of fuzzy and confusing at this point.

ACTION ITEM

Listen to Lee Cockerell, the former Executive Vice President of Walt Disney World who once managed 40,000 employees

https://www. ThrivetimeShow.com/ business-podcasts/ disney-magic-how-lee-cockerell-managed-40000-employees-1-million-customers-and-himself/

STEP 1 -
Only eat meat.

STEP 2 -
Only drink coffee or water.

STEP 3 -
Don't eat anything
other than meat.

STEP 4 -
Don't drink anything other
than coffee or water.

Quick Note:

*You should be at a place in your
entrepreneurial journey where you
recognize that if you can't sell your
business will not do well.*

FUN FACT: CLAY CLARK'S THRIVETIMESHOW PODCAST
HAS HIT #1 ON THE ITUNES PODCAST CHART SIX TIMES

NOTABLE QUOTABLE

"To know thyself is the beginning of wisdom."

» **SOCRATES**

(A classical Greek philosopher who was credited as being one of the founders of modern Western Philosophy.)

*"IF YOU'RE GOING TO BE THINKING ANYTHING,
YOU MIGHT AS WELL THINK BIG."
– DONALD TRUMP*

(Real Estate Mogul, Author, the man behind the TRUMP brands, and the 45th President of the United States.)

"SOME PEOPLE DIE AT 25 AND AREN'T BURIED UNTIL 75."
- BENJAMIN FRANKLIN

(An American polymath who was one of the Founding
Fathers of the United States. During his ti me,
Benjamin Franklin was a renowned author, politi cian,
scienti st, inventor and diplomat. He alone convinced
the French to supply the United States with the
ammuniti on and weapons needed to win the war
against the Briti sh as the colonists faced certain
defeat without the French support.)

FUN FACT: CLAY CLARK'S THRIVETIMESHOW PODCAST
HAS HIT #1 ON THE ITUNES PODCAST CHART SIX TIMES

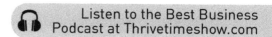

DAY 20

REFUSE TO MANAGE LATE-ARRIVING, LOW-ENERGY, & NEFARIOUS PEOPLE

. . . .

When it comes to human resources, nothing works unless you and your employees do. You simply do not have enough time to spend your day managing late-arriving, low-energy and nefarious people.

I'll never forget. While we were growing The Elephant In The Room Men's Grooming Lounge I had to ask a man if he was sleeping with a team member that he was managing while he was still married to his wife? He said yes and he was shocked why I had to let him go.

I'll never forget. While we were growing The Elephant In The Room Men's Grooming Lounge I had to ask a man if he was using the company credit card to buy lingerie and expensive dates? He said yes and he was shocked why I had to let him go.

I'll never forget. While we were growing The Elephant In The Room Men's Grooming Lounge I had to ask a man if he was using company money to buy a massive truck? He said yes and he was shocked why I had to let him go.

I'll never forget. While we were growing The Elephant In The Room Men's Grooming Lounge I had to ask a man if he was taking cash out the register and not reporting it? He said yes and he was shocked why I had to let him go.

I'll never forget. While we were growing The Elephant In The Room Men's Grooming Lounge I had to ask a man if it would be possible for him to EVER show up to on-time for the management meeting? He said he would try, and he was shocked why I had to let him go.

When you are dealing with this low level of productivity killing jackassery on a daily basis you just simply don't have enough left in your day to be successful. You must hire great people and fire the idiots.

NOTABLE QUOTABLE WORTH REPEATING

"Face reality as it is, not as it was or as you wish it to be."

» **JACK WELCH**

(The CEO who grew GE by 4,000% during his tenure.)

NOTABLE QUOTABLE

"²⁷ Idle hands are the devil's workshop; idle lips are his mouthpiece. ²⁸ An evil man sows strife; gossip separates the best of friends. ²⁹ Wickedness loves company—and leads others into sin."

» **PROVERBS 16:27-29**

Today, you must rate yourself in the following areas and do it NOW (with 10 being the highest)!

How would you rate your ability to hire, inspire, & retain quality employees on a scale of 1 - 10?

1   2   3   4   5   6   7   8   9   10

Do you post weekly on Indeed.com, Craigslist, etc.?

_____

Do you have a scripted job posting?

_____

Do you conduct weekly interviews?

_____

Do you have a scripted interview process?

_____

You Must Keep the Following Facts In Your Mind As You Engage In the Accounting Grind:

"75% of employees steal from the workplace."

> » **U.S. Chamber of Commerce**
>
> https://www.cbsnews.com/news/employee-theft-are-you-blind-to-it/

"85 Percent of Job Applicants Lie on Resumes."

> » **Inc Magazine**
>
> https://www.inc.com/jt-odonnell/staggering-85-of-job-applicants-lying-on-resumes-.html

DEFINITIONS MATTER:

. . . .

Abdicate:

Abdicate implies a giving up of sovereign power or sometimes an evading of responsibility such as that of a parent.

DEFINITIONS MATTER:

Delegate:

Assigning an action item to someone and following up until the desired results are delivered with excellence.

 You must install a merit-based pay system and when possible remove any kind of salaries that are not attached to work performance.

 You must install daily huddles with your staff.

 You must install a weekly group interview to interview new employee candidates at the same time each week.

 You must install a weekly recurring staff training / team meeting that will proactively prevent and solve any human resource problems.

 You must schedule a weekly 1 hour meeting with your team to coach them up and teach them new skills. Listen to this podcast to learn more about the importance of having a weekly time booked on a recurring basis to train your team. SETTING UP A WEEKLY TIME TO TRAIN YOUR TEAM (3 HOURS PER WEEK)

 » https://www.thrivetimeshow.com/business-podcasts/setting-up-a-weekly-time-to-train-your-team-3-hours-per-week/

You must write a compelling job post for Indeed and other job posting websites.

You must write a pre-written email response to potential candidates.

You must schedule a weekly time to conduct the Group Interview - Listen to the following podcast - **HOW TO SET UP A WEEKLY GROUP INTERVIEW PROCESS**

» https://www.thrivetimeshow.com/business-podcasts/set-weekly-group-interview-process/

You must write a script for the group interview process. Listen to the following podcast **THE GROUP INTERVIEW – THIS IS HOW WE DO IT – A KNOWLEDGE BOMB** -

» https://www.thrivetimeshow.com/business-podcasts/the-group-interview-this-is-how-we-do-it-a-knowledge-bomb/

You must schedule a weekly time to launch the "now hiring" job posts on Craigslist and Indeed. Listen to this podcast to learn more about how to retain quality staff. **HOW TO RETAIN QUALITY STAFF**

» https://www.thrivetimeshow.com/business-podcasts/retain-quality-staff/

You must listen to this podcast to get comfortable with the concept of how to interview job candidates: **THE GROUP INTERVIEW – THIS IS HOW WE DO IT – A KNOWLEDGE BOMB**

> » https://www.thrivetimeshow.com/business-podcasts/the-group-interview-this-is-how-we-do-it-a-knowledge-bomb/

Listen to the following podcast to learn how to hire, inspire, train and retain high-quality employees. How to Hire Quality Humans On the Planet Earth + Human Resources 101 | Nothing Will Work Unless They Do | How to Hire, Inspire, Train & Retain Quality People + Outwitting the Devil by Sharon Lechter

> » WATCH - https://rumble.com/v4fa3v0-business-podcasts-how-to-hire-quality-humans.html

When managing real people on the real planet Earth you must embrace the reality of today's employees:

Do you remember when childhood was supposed to be about exploration, love, and innocence? They don't.

A study put together in 2006 by the Centers for Disease Control and Prevention showed that 1 in 4 women and 1 in 6 men were sexually abused before the age of 18. This means there are more than 42 million adult survivors of child sexual abuse in the United States.

LEARN HOW TO START AND GROW A BUSINESS BY LISTENING TO THE THRIVETIMESHOW.COM PODCAST TODAY!

231

Did your father ever tell you what it meant to be a man or a woman?

THEIR FATHERS DIDN'T.

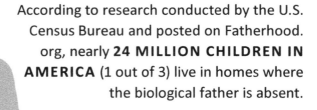

According to research conducted by the U.S. Census Bureau and posted on Fatherhood. org, nearly **24 MILLION CHILDREN IN AMERICA** (1 out of 3) live in homes where the biological father is absent.

According to a study done by the Fulton County Texas Department of Corrections, **85% OF ALL YOUTHS IN PRISON** come from fatherless homes. Thus, kids who come from fatherless homes are nearly 20 times more likely to go to jail than kids who were raised in a home with their biological fathers.

According to a September 1988 study by the United States Department of Justice, **70% OF YOUTHS IN STATE-OPERATED INSTITUTIONS** come from fatherless homes — 9 times the average.

Did you ever get in trouble with your parents for not studying hard and doing well on your tests?

THEY NEVER DID.

In a 2011 article written by Lory Hough, the Harvard School of Education found that over **50% OF THE 18-24 YEAR OLD AMERICANS** surveyed by National Geographic couldn't find the state of New York on a map.

In a Sept 14, 2011 article posted by Michael Winter for USA Today, the College Board now shows that just **40% OF THE HIGH SCHOOL SENIORS** met benchmarks for college success.

Did your parents ever teach you about the consequences of your actions?

THEIR PARENTS NEVER DID.

In a May of 2008 article published in USA Today, researchers in Chicago found that **1 IN 4 TEEN GIRLS** have a sexually transmitted disease. Thus, approximately 3 million teens now have an STD.

In a March 9th, 2012 article posted on Reuters by JoAnne Allen, about **16% OF AMERICANS BETWEEN THE AGES OF 14 AND 49** are infected with genital herpes, making it one of the most common sexually transmitted diseases.

In Newsweek's cover story entitled "iCrazy", it was revealed that one quarter of employees who use the internet **DURING WORK VISIT PORN SITES**. In fact, hits to porn sites are highest during office hours than at any other time of day.

Did your parents ever teach you that a quitter never wins and that a winner never quits?

THEIR PARENTS NEVER DID.

Despite being in a deep economic recession, a July 7th, 2010 article published by the Harvard Business Review reported that **MORE EMPLOYEES QUIT THEIR JOBS** than were terminated, according to the US Bureau of Labor Statistics 3 month research.

Do you remember when college was supposed to make you more intelligent and more hirable?

THEY DON'T.

According to a USA Today Article written by Mary Beth Marklein, research shows students spent **50% LESS TIME STUDYING** compared with students a few decades ago. The research compared college students enrolled in 2001 versus college students enrolled in 2011.

Whatever happened to common sense?

According to Gail Cunningham, In a 2011 Newsweek Article, research was conducted by asking 1,000 U.S. citizens to take America's official citizenship test. **TWENTY NINE PERCENT (29%) COULDN'T NAME THE VICE PRESIDENT**. Seventy-three percent couldn't correctly explain why we fought the Cold War.

As quoted in a July 2012 article in Newsweek Magazine, **56% OF U.S. ADULTS ADMIT THEY DON'T HAVE A BUDGET**; one-third don't pay all their bills on time.

According to an article written by Mary Beth Marklein in USA Today, nearly half of the nation's undergraduates show almost no gains in learning in their first two years of college. The report concludes this is because, in large part, colleges don't make academics a priority. Among their top activities, students report spending **24% OF THEIR TIME SLEEPING**, 51% of their time socializing and just 7% actually studying.

If you work hard and commit yourself to excellence anyone can obtain the American dream.

BUT WHAT IF YOU DON'T WANT TO WORK HARD?

According to Gail Cunningham, In a 2011 Newsweek Article, research was conducted by asking 1,000 U.S. citizens to take America's official citizenship test. **TWENTY NINE PERCENT (29%) COULDN'T NAME THE VICE PRESIDENT**. Seventy-three percent couldn't correctly explain why we fought the Cold War.

As quoted in a July 2012 article in Newsweek Magazine, **56% OF U.S. ADULTS ADMIT THEY DON'T HAVE A BUDGET**; one-third don't pay all their bills on time.

According to an article written by Mary Beth Marklein in USA Today, nearly half of the nation's undergraduates show almost no gains in learning in their first two years of college. The report concludes this is because, in large part, colleges don't make academics a priority. Among their top activities, students report spending **24% OF THEIR TIME SLEEPING**, 51% of their time socializing and just 7% actually studying.

FREE BONUS TIP:

"Nothing will work unless you do."

» **MAYA ANGELOU**

(Poet, producer, actress and prolific writer.)

Do you remember what it was like to converse with someone who wasn't updating their Facebook status and texting while waiting for you to finish speaking?

THEY DON'T.

According to research conducted by Research Basex and reported in a February issue of USA Today, "productivity losses due to the **COST OF UNNECESSARY INTERRUPTIONS**" were at $650 billion in 2007.

In a 2002 article published by New York Times Best-Selling Author Ken Blanchard, a large survey of **1,300 PRIVATE-SECTOR COMPANIES**, conducted by Proudfoot Consulting, found that on average only 59% of work time is productive.

A March 2, 2011 study published by Inc. Magazine shows employees are **UNPRODUCTIVE FOR HALF OF THE DAY**.

In an article posted by Martha C. White on March 13th, 2012 entitled, "You're Wasting Time at Work Right Now, Aren't You?" revealed that a 2012 study of 3,200 employees conducted by Salary.com showed that **64% SAY THEY VISIT WEBSITES** unrelated to work daily.

Do you remember when 1 out of 5 of your co-workers wasn't insane?

THEY DON'T.

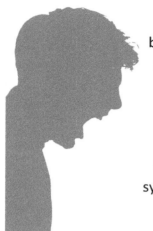

According to a disturbing article published by Harvard Health Publications in February of 2010, researchers analyzing results from the U.S. The National Comorbidity Survey found a nationally representative study of Americans ages 15 to 54. In that study it was reported that **18% OF THOSE WHO WERE EMPLOYED** said they experienced symptoms of a mental health disorder in the previous month.

I think it's a good idea to bring up the whole Carnivore Diet thing again. If you are going to be successful in business you must learn to embrace the core repeatable actionable processes that have been proven to work. Yes, you must embrace the C.R.A.P. You must embrace those Core Repeatable Actionable Processes that have been proven to work. However, they will be repetitive and they will be proven work. The greats among us bore down while most mediocre people struggle with boredom. Keep that in mind.

And here is a quick recap of the Carnivore Diet in case you forgot:

STEP 1 -

Only eat meat.

STEP 2 -

Only drink coffee or water.

STEP 3 -

Don't eat anything other than meat.

STEP 4 -

Don't drink anything other than coffee or water.

Work with your coach to develop a merit-based pay system for your team based upon paying people for what they do vs. what they say they are going to do.

Position:

_____

Pay:

_____

Metric / Key Performance Indicators:

_____

Carrot:

_____

Stick:

_____

Quick Note:

Remember, if you don't sell anything you aren't in business, you are in poverty causing busyness.

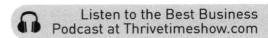

DAY 21

NEVER DELEGATE YOUR FINANCIALS TO ANYONE OTHER THAN YOURSELF, OR YOUR BUSINESS WILL GO TO HELL!

. . . .

Accounting for your business is like keeping score in the game of basketball, football, baseball or volleyball. You must keep score so that you know if you are winning or not. Take a moment and write down the answers to the following questions.

How proactive is your accounting on a scale of 1 - 10 (with 10 being the highest)?

1   2   3   4   5   6   7   8   9   10

Do you have a documented break-even number?

Yes   No

Do you have a process for proactively setting enough aside for taxes?

Yes   No

Do you automate your savings?

Yes   No

Do you have a documented and updated report of your income and expenses?

Yes   No

Do you have a set time and place to review your finances every week?

Yes   No

NOTABLE QUOTABLE

"In fact, what determines your wealth is not how much you make but how much you keep of what you make."

» **DAVID BACH**

(*New York Times* best-selling author of *Automatic Millionaire.*)

FUN FACT: CLAY CLARK'S THRIVETIMESHOW PODCAST HAS HIT #1 ON THE ITUNES PODCAST CHART SIX TIMES

Fun Facts Worth Repeating: This just in.... Most people in your business are lying, cheating, and stealing.

"75% of employees steal from the workplace."

» **U.S. Chamber of Commerce**

https://www.cbsnews.com/news/employee-theft-are-you-blind-to-it/

"85 Percent of Job Applicants Lie on Resumes."

» **Inc Magazine**

https://www.inc.com/jt-odonnell/staggering-85-of-job-applicants-lying-on-resumes-.html

DEFINITIONS MATTER:

Abdicate:

Abdicate implies a giving up of sovereign power or sometimes an evading of responsibility such as that of a parent.

LEARN HOW TO START AND GROW A BUSINESS BY LISTENING TO THE THRIVETIMESHOW.COM PODCAST TODAY!

243

INSTALL A MERIT-BASED PAY SYSTEM in your business so that nobody gets paid unless you do. Remove any salaries that allow people to get paid without delivering service, value and accountability.

Create an income / expenses sheet featuring the following areas:

- Monthly Hard Costs (Fixed costs that do not change)

- Monthly Variable Costs (Costs per transaction)

- Monthly Income

Determine to save a set percentage of your income.

Schedule a recurring weekly two hour block per week (minimum) to look at your numbers.

- Assume everyone is lying, cheating, steal and is perpetually wrong about basic math.

- Look for deviations that don't seem accurate, consistent or normal.

» **Listen the podcast on how to design a sustainable schedule** - https://www.ThrivetimeShow.com/thrive-time-show/f6-life-learning-design-life-want-ep-228/

ACTION ITEM - Listen to best-selling author and author of the Rich Dad Poor Dad Sharon Lechter teach why you can't delegate financials and cash flow 101 -

 https://www.ThrivetimeShow.com/business-podcasts/rich-dad-poor-dad-author-sharon-lechter-teaches-why-you-cant-delegate-financials-and-cash-flow-101/

 ACTION ITEM - Listen to the podcast on how to create an effective proforma

 https://www.ThrivetimeShow.com/business-podcasts/creating-a-detailed-proforma-for-your-business/

 ACTION ITEM - Determine if you have enough insurance in place to keep you from having a bad life and not just a bad day when things go wrong

 https://www.ThrivetimeShow.com/business-podcasts/need-buy-liability-insurance/

 ACTION ITEM - Listen to How to Manage the Payroll & Accounting of a Business | Abdicate Vs. Delegate, the Path to Successful Payroll Processing + "Why You Can't Delegate Financials & Cashflow."

» Workman's compensation insurance

» General liability insurance

» Supplemental insurance (Insurance that pays you on a daily basis in the event that you are not able to work)

» Auto insurance

» Umbrella insurance - Liability insurance that is purchased to cover any gaps in your insurance not covered by the other insurance policies that you have in place.

» Property insurance

» Health insurance

- Sharon Lechter, CPA
(Co-author of *Rich Dad Poor Dad*)

 WATCH - https://rumble.com/v4f9ycw-business-how-to-manage-the-payroll-and-accounting-of-a.html

Because I am not the best-selling co-author of the number one business book of our generation I wanted to allow the best-selling co-author of *Rich Dad, Poor Dad* and the legendary CPA, Sharon Lechter to teach you about business accounting. So, listed below is a transcript from one of my interviews with Sharon Lechter. Sharon Lechter is a CPA, entrepreneur, philanthropist, mother and the co-author of the *New York Times* best-selling *Rich Dad, Poor Dad* book series which went on to sell 23 million copies. She served as former CEO of the Rich Dad Organization and sold the first million copies of *Rich Dad, Poor Dad* while the organization was still based in her home. In 2008, Sharon was asked by the Napoleon Hill Foundation to join the team to co-author multiple book projects including the best-sellers: *Think and Grow Rich-Three Feet from Gold, Outwitting the Devil, Think and Grow Rich for Women,* and *Grow Rich for Kids.*

ONE OF THE THINGS THAT YOU WRITE ABOUT IN YOUR BOOKS IS THE IMPORTANCE OF BUYING ASSETS WHENEVER POSSIBLE AND AVOIDING LIABILITIES AT ALL COST. WHAT DO YOU CONSIDER AN ASSET AND WHAT DO YOU CONSIDER TO BE A LIABILITY?

"What liabilities do you have? Well, for those of you familiar with the *Rich Dad, Poor Dad*, we talked about assets signed up being things that put money in your pocket. Liabilities are the things that take money out of your pocket. Assets feed you, liabilities eat you. At the end of the day, that's true. In *Rich Dad, Poor Dad*, we talk about how your house is not an asset— why? Because it doesn't make you money."

» **SHARON LECHTER**

Your house is not an asset because it does not make you money.

"It's something you have to pay for, so we want you to create enough assets that are feeding you. We want assets that are generating income that can pay for the house you want. Don't look at your house as your bank account. You want to have those businesses, you want to build businesses, you want to have real estate. Obviously, people have intellectual property which is the greatest way to build assets because that comes from your mind. Writing books, solving problems, serving needs. When you come up with something unique and have the opportunity to protect it, that's a patent. That is something that can earn you money for years and years and years through licensing. If you don't want to build your own business around it, license it to someone else, and those assets continue to build, grow, and make you money when you're sleeping.

That's the thing when they talk about rental real estate being mailbox money. It takes a lot of energy up front to find the properties, and get them going. Then you have to find a management company, which is not quite as much of a headache on a long-term basis. Now in real estate, there are different types of real estate investments. An asset earns money while you are sleeping.

There is Fix and Flip - that takes a lot more energy and that's really not passive income. Then there's the long term cashflow play where you buy and hold and have rental properties. In that case you have tenants who are paying your rent, and the debt to buy those properties is good debt.

As long as what they're paying you in rent exceeds all the related expenses and your monthly mortgage payment, you're getting cash flow positive. That's something that is an asset, it is good debt. You need to look at each category of debt you have, and say, how is this going to help me move forward? Is this going to generate an asset for me? Is this going to sustain an asset? At the end of the day, most people talk about work-life balance, but it is not really work-life balance, it is debt-life balance. People have too much bad debt and that is keeping them from living the life they deserve. Income you earn passively exceeds the income."

» **SHARON LECHTER**

There is a quote,

"The class of people who control their environmental influences are the non-drifters. All who are victims of the habit of drifting forfeit their power to choose their own environment. They become the victims of every negative influence of their environment."

Why is it so important to control your environment and what does it even mean? From my personal experience I do also believe that 98% of the people I've met are drifters.

"Part of that is what are you allowing in your space? Are you putting yourself in a group of people who want you to succeed? Are they there to support you and encourage you? Or are you putting yourself around people who basically want to keep you in your place? If you start to make an improvement, will they want to pull you back? The environment is everything. It's so important to understand what you're feeding your mind as well as knowing you need to support yourself. In that concept of the non-drifters, think of the term 'go with the flow'. Drifters, which Napoleon Hill says take up about 98% of the population, are the ones who basically don't make plans. They don't have that definiteness of purpose. A non-drifter knows what they want out of life. They have a definite purpose, and they create a plan to get what they want. They don't let other people divert them. Certainly, they get off the path every once in a while, but they know what their goal is, so they recalibrate, refocus, and start moving forward.

The drifters basically say, well whatever you want or go with the flow, and they flow right off the hill. You might know a drifter in your life who you've tried to help. You know that they're lost, and you talked until you were blue in the face, and they didn't respond. I would always recommend giving them the gift of the book *Outwitting the Devil*, because, they may very well find themselves in that book. They might find that lifeline of hope that will help them find that definiteness of purpose in their own life."

» **SHARON LECHTER**

WHY DO YOU THINK THAT PEOPLE DON'T TRY TO GROW OR SCALE?

"Be careful about helping too many drifters. They will steal your energy and your time and you will somehow end up feeling that you did not do enough to help them.

Well, sometimes we get in a world of comfort and that comfort turns into complacency. Even though we're not where we want to be, we're able to pay our bills and put our head on the pillow at night, we end up getting too comfortable. What happens is a lot of times we have a crisis and we get thrown into chaos, and we end up having to become creative again. That gives us the ability to have a bigger vision and reevaluate the whole concept of what's possible. I think a huge issue is your environment, are you hanging out with other people that are in that same category? Or, are you spending your time with people who are just getting by, and people who are in the rat race? If that's the environment you're putting yourself in, then it seems normal, right?

If you want to get out of that environment, then you need to put yourself in an environment with people who are really striving for success. They can help you. Most of the time we are taught, certainly in school, to do it on our own. We come out in the business world and we think we have to do everything on our own. It's so important that we realize that if you have the right people around you, the right team, the right peer network, you'll have the opportunity to grow more quickly. Mentors are priceless because they have already been successful, they are already where you want to go, and they can help speed your way to success by opening doors, and steering you around the pitfalls. There's a difference between a mentor and a coach. A coach may not have that success, but they know what you want to do, and they can help you be accountable and make sure you stay on track. Are you mostly learning from mentors or mistakes?"

» **SHARON LECHTER**

MOST PEOPLE SEEM TO GET STUCK IN THE SELF EMPLOYED AREA, WHY IS THAT?

"Well, I think a lot of times you start getting so busy working in your business you forget to work ON your business. People feel like they have to do everything on their own, and they don't bring in the talent to help them grow their business. In order to be able to grow from a small business to a big business, you have to have systems. When you do everything yourself, it is going to be hard to grow. Nobody's ever going to do it exactly the way you want, unless you create the systems. Obviously, we can think of the most perfect example: McDonald's is everywhere. The owner is not there, so they're run by teenagers. It's done like that because the systems are so ironclad that all that somebody has to do is follow the systems. That's the idea of going from a small business to a big business. A big business has systems and you manage the systems, not necessarily the people. You have people working for you, your systems are working for you and other people's money. That's what really gets you out of a small business to a large business. Now, maybe as a small business, you're a doctor or you're a lawyer, so how do you do that? Well, you hire other doctors or other lawyers and you start building a practice around it, so that you have the ability to earn. You need to have systems.

To know how the operations are being handled, and you make a percentage off the other create scalable doctors and lawyers. You're taking the overhead and you have the ability to grow and leverage. You might have a very successful small business, but a successful systems small business can only scale, and therefore be sustainable, if it has systems. "

» **SHARON LECHTER**

WHY CAN'T YOU ABDICATE YOUR FINANCIALS AS THE OWNER OF A COMPANY? WHY IS IT SO IMPORTANT TO BE AWARE OF WHAT'S GOING ON FINANCIALLY?

"At the end of the day, your numbers tell a story and you're creating that story. If your story isn't going the way you want it to go, the sooner you know about it, the better. This is very important for entrepreneurs. You can't be the one doing the numbers because you want to focus on growing your business.

However, you do need to make sure you have the right people on your team. This does not mean you can ignore your numbers. I would suggest a dashboard, or something so that you are constantly on.

As I sit at my desk right now, I have my accountants outside working on some things for me. They know that at any given time, I need to know what kind of accounts I have. I know what kind of money I have just because of my years of experience. As a CPA, that's obviously important to me, but it's more important to me as a CEO. If you own your company, if you don't know what the numbers are telling you then you can get a rude surprise. It's crucial for people to understand the importance of being able to interpret the income statement, which is telling you over a

FUN FACT: CLAY CLARK'S THRIVETIMESHOW PODCAST HAS HIT #1 ON THE ITUNES PODCAST CHART SIX TIMES

period of time how you're doing. You also should understand your balance sheet, which basically gives you a snapshot of a day and time, showing you what your assets and liabilities are. How those two play together is very important."

» **SHARON LECHTER**

EVERY ENTREPRENEUR MUST KNOW:

MONTHLY GROSS REVENUE	**MONTHLY EXPENSES**	**MONTHLY PROFIT**	**MONTHLY NUMBER OF NEW CUSTOMERS**

COULD YOU GIVE US THE TOUGH LOVE FOR SOMEBODY WHO IS REFUSING TO KNOW THEIR NUMBERS?

"90% of startup businesses fail in the first 3 years. Well, they know that 90% of businesses fail in the first three years, and the primary reason they fail is lack of capital, funding, and financial management. What happens is those entrepreneurs that fall into that category are the ones who put their head in the sand. They think that if they just drive faster and they make more sales, everything is going to be okay. The issue is, unless you understand the whole picture and what your margins are, and understand what the bottom line is, you can't really grow your business.

People that are losing a nickel on an item will say, 'If I can just sell more of them, I'll be okay.' No, you're just going to lose that

LEARN HOW TO START AND GROW A BUSINESS BY LISTENING TO THE THRIVETIMESHOW.COM PODCAST TODAY!

253

much more money. You have to understand the cash flow of your business, and more importantly, you need to understand the timing of your cash flow.

It's not just understanding that you sell a lot, but you need to understand when that money is coming in, and when you have to spend money in order to make the product. So, let's say you sell a million dollars worth of product. You have to have that product in your inventory, or you have to have the money to build it, so that you can collect a million dollars. You probably need a lot of that cash upfront."

» **SHARON LECHTER**

USING BUILDING A HOUSE AS AN EXAMPLE, WHAT IS CASH FLOW AND WHAT DO WE NEED TO DO ABOUT IT?

"Well, building a house is a perfect example of the timing of cash flow that I just mentioned. You don't build a house overnight. You have to have the financing to get that house built, knowing that the payoff is in the future. When that payoff comes in, hopefully it's going to not only pay off your expenses but it gives you the profit on top of it. Those expenses include all those materials and the labor of all the people on your team. When I talk about cash flow, I want to take a minute about materials. We talk about 'just in time' ordering, so when you're building that house, you have to put the plumbing in before they can pour the concrete over it. There's an order in which you have things done. You can't have the roofers waiting to put the roof on when it's not ready for them, and so each stage or process of building the home has to be timed appropriately. That way you have the minimum cost of labor for the people and the technicians doing their job. That has to be perfectly timed, so it takes talent and people who know what they're doing. It also takes that expert in that or individual understanding what every minute of that costs them, so when they have a delay they are able to recalculate, and find out what that's going to cost them. Then they can make sure that they're always working inside their budget, and they will have the profit that they're expecting at the end of the day.

We talk about remodels as the homeowner right? You always say it's always going to take another several months past what they promise as a guarantee and it's going to cost you more than what you originally committed to because you're going to have surprises and that's something that can be very painful, but that's those unexpected things. Every business has unexpected things. The issue is, the sooner you find out about them, the sooner you can plan and recover, and that's all about cash flow. Cash flow comes from the moment you start your business. One of the things that can kill you is that you think you have sales and the sales are there, but it's going to take you 60 to 90 days to collect on those sales. You have to have the cash to be able to build the product. What happens when all of a sudden you are hugely successful and you have a huge order that comes in and you don't have the ability to respond to that order. Your business can crumble. That's why it's so important to always have a pulse on your cash flow, not just your income and expenses, but also the cash flow, which is the timing of that. That's why when fortune 500 companies do an income statement, or balance sheet, and a cash flow statement so that you can see what's happening within the business."

» **SHARON LECHTER**

WHY ARE YOU SO PASSIONATE ABOUT A FINANCIAL LITERACY WHEN YOU COULD HAVE OBVIOUSLY COULD HAVE BEEN DONE YEARS AGO?

"What would it feel like to be truly financially free? I've been financially free for 20 years, it's never been about the money. Growing up as a little child, my father would ask me each night if I added value to someone's life, and I still ask that. I lost him in 2006, but I continue to feel that each of us has a responsibility to support others. I think that I have a gift and a responsibility because of my ability to teach people about money. I can show them how to change their mindsets about money, how to go from scarcity thinking to abundance, and realizing that the opportunity is there. All we need to do is you just need to learn how to teach ourselves to recognize it, seize it, and take action.

What I'm doing this year with the Play Big movement is really coming back to focus on what I want to do. I really thought about retiring last year, and it didn't sit too well with me. I said, "you know I've been given a gift and an opportunity and as long as I can continue supporting people taking control of their financial lives, that's what I want to do."

» **SHARON LECHTER**

Hey look we are approaching the end of this life-changing book and I bet you now know alot about how to start and grow a successful business and you probably know alot about the four main variables involved in the Carnivore Diet. However, in case you need a refresher.

STEP 1 -
Only eat meat.

STEP 2 -
Only drink coffee or water.

STEP 3 -
Don't eat anything other than meat.

STEP 4 -
Don't drink anything other than coffee or water.

Quick Note:

As an entrepreneur you must develop a quick-bias and focus for selling products and services to your ideal and likely buyers in exchange for a profit or you may end up going back to college and racking up more student debt while studying business class from a professor who doesn't know how to run a business.

LEARN HOW TO START AND GROW A BUSINESS BY LISTENING TO THE THRIVETIMESHOW.COM PODCAST TODAY!

257

"CONTROL YOUR OWN DESTINY OR
SOMEONE ELSE WILL."
— JACK WELCH

(The CEO who grew GE by 4,000% during his tenure.)

FUN FACT: CLAY CLARK'S THRIVETIMESHOW PODCAST
HAS HIT #1 ON THE ITUNES PODCAST CHART SIX TIMES

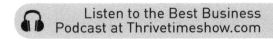

DAY 22

ACTION. ACTION. ACTION.

. . . .

You, my friend, now know what you need to do. However, the legendary best-selling author of *Think & Grow Rich* was 100% correct when he once wrote, "**ACTION IS THE REAL MEASURE OF INTELLIGENCE.**" - **Napoleon Hill** (The best-selling author of *Think & Grow Rich*).

Remember, what gets scheduled gets done and this life is not a dress rehearsal. Now get out there and turn your dreams into reality!!! It seems like we may have covered it, but the main four variables involved in this thing called the Carnivore Diet are:

STEP 1 -
Only eat meat.

STEP 2 -
Only drink coffee or water.

STEP 3 -
Don't eat anything other than meat.

STEP 4 -
Don't drink anything other than coffee or water.

NOTABLE QUOTABLE

"Education is the key to unlock the golden door of freedom."

» GEORGE WASHINGTON CARVER

(The famous botanist who was born a slave and went on to completely revolutionize the way Americans farm.)

Quick Note:

Are you aware that if your income does not exceed your expenses you will quickly go into bankruptcy?

Printed in the USA
CPSIA information can be obtained
at www.ICGtesting.com
LVHW051941080924
790210LV00020B/330